INTERNATIONAL GUIDELINES ON OPEN AND DISTANCE TEACHER EDUCATION

INTERNATIONAL GUIDELINES ON OPEN AND DISTANCE TEACHER EDUCATION

Editor

Dr. Digumarti Bhaskara Rao

M.Sc., M.A., M.A., M.Ed., Ph.D.,

Secretary

Academy of Communication Culture

Education Science and Service

Guntur–522 006

Andhra Pradesh

India

DISCOVERY PUBLISHING HOUSE

NEW DELHI-110002

First Published - 2004

Reprinted - 2014

ISBN: 978-81-7141-777-3

International Guidelines on Open and Distance Teacher Education

Published by:

DISCOVERY PUBLISHING HOUSE PVT. LTD.
4383/4B, Ansari Road, Darya Ganj
New Delhi-110 002 (India)
Phone: +91-11-23279245, 43596064-65
Fax: +91-11-23253475
E-mail: discoverypublishinghouse@gmail.com
sales@discoverypublishinggroup.com
web: www.discoverypublishinggroup.com

Printed at:
Infinity Imaging Systems
Delhi

Preface

The international guidelines on teacher education are intended for the policy planners, educational officers, academic administrators, and heads of teacher education institutions and others who are concerned with the expansion and implementation of open and distance learning in teacher education.

The guidelines try to answer eight major questions related to the open and distance learning for teachers, such as—what is wrong with teacher education?, is distance education relevant?, what has it been used for?, how is it planned and managed?, what technologies can we use?, how can you fund it?, how do teachers learn practical skills?, how can we assess it? and many more minor questions, and to identify the options available to planners and strategies for choosing among the options in the light of the answers to them.

These guidelines are developed based on the experiences in teacher education; the case studies undertaken on behalf of UNESCO in Brazil, Burkina Faso, Chile, China, India, Mongolia, Nigeria, South Africa and United Kingdom; and several other international studies.

The guidelines on open and distance teacher education appeared in this book are reproduced from the UNESCO publications entitled 'Teacher Education Guidelines: Using Open and Distance Learning—Technology Curriculum Cost Evaluation' and 'Teacher Education through Distance Learning—Technology Curriculum Evaluation Cost', both written by Hilary Perraton, Charlotte Creed and Bernadette Robinson. Ratimir Kvaternik extended UNESCO editorial co-ordination.

I am very much thankful to all the educationists involved in the development of these guidelines, and grateful to the UNESCO for reproducing the material from its publications for the benefit of the teacher education community.

Dr. Digumarti Bhaskara Rao

Contents

What is Wrong with Teacher Education?

Teachers are vital. Unless we can get more teachers, and better teachers, we will not reach the target of making quality education available for all by 2015. But there are still world shortages of teachers, still large numbers of under-qualified teachers, and still many who need further professional education and training as they work. Conventional approaches to teacher education have not met all the demands upon the profession and this has led to an interest in open and distance learning alternatives.

In much of the south and especially in sub-Saharan Africa and South Asia, problems of teacher supply, of four kinds, threaten the attainment of the education targets.

First, there are shortages of teachers. While school enrolments generally grew in the 1990s, teacher numbers only just kept pace with them; indeed, in six Commonwealth African countries pupil numbers were growing faster than teacher numbers. Meanwhile, AIDS is reducing the life expectancy of teachers and so increasing the numerical demands. With all the other pressures on educational budgets, it seems unlikely that teachers' colleges can be expanded at the rate necessary to meet these demands. Teacher shortages continue to dominate the educational landscape.

Second, in many but not all countries female teachers are in a minority in primary schools. Progress in getting more women into the profession is slow; in Africa the proportion of women rose from 39.4 per cent to 43.3 per cent between 1990 and 1997, while in south Asia it rose only from 28 to 29.6 per cent.

Third, even where there are enough teachers, too many of them are untrained or undertrained, and the quality of training is often itself inadequate. A number of studies have found little difference between the effectiveness of trained and untrained teachers. 'About half of the teachers in developing countries are unqualified in terms of their own country's formal standards for teachers' education. Many teachers have little more than secondary education themselves. Teaching methods are often old fashioned, with too much focus on rote learning' (DFID 2001: 9).

Fourth, in many countries, there is a national desire not just to raise the quality of the teaching force to match the present demands on them but also to change teachers' jobs as their host societies are changing. New goals create new demands: gender parity by 2005 and universal basic education by 2015; inclusive education; education for democracy, peace and social cohesion; multi-grade teaching; increased accountability for achieving learning targets; the development of learners who are self-managing and independent, skilled in critical thinking and problem solving, equipped with life-skills; the preparation of learners who are competent for knowledge-based economies, capable in the use of information technology; and the expansion of teachers' roles to include social work in communities where child-headed households and orphans are common as a result of HIV-AIDS. In transition countries, society is expecting teachers to change their approach as education itself is being reformed, within the context of social change. And these changes in role and changes in expectation are likely to affect both the initial education of teachers and programmes of continuing professional development.

All of this creates new challenges for teacher education and continuing professional development: the need to find ways of using existing resources differently, an expanding access to learning opportunities at affordable cost, of providing alternative pathways to initial teacher training, of drawing on new constituencies of the population to work as teachers, of using technologies appropriately to enrich teaching and support practice, of stimulating and supporting teachers' active learning and of reconceptualising the traditional organisation of initial teacher education and continuing progressional development.

In order to make good planning decisions about teacher education we need to ask in turn: what does it consist of? Who are the teachers? and what is the curriculum?

What does it consist of?

Teacher education has to do a whole range of different jobs: to enable teachers to develop the potential of their pupils; to serve as role models; to help transform education and through it society; to encourage self-confidence and creativity. At the same time, many educators often hope that student teachers will develop appropriate, and where necessary changed, attitudes to their job. In order to meet these hopes, teacher education is likely to include four elements: improving the general educational background of the trainee teachers; increasing their knowledge and understanding of the subjects they are to teach; pedagogy and understanding of children and learning; and the development of practical skills and competences.

The balance between these four elements varies in relation to the background education of student teachers, to the level at which they will teach, and to the stage they have reached in their career. Two distinctions are important here. The first is between the initial education and training of teachers and their continuing professional development. The second is between pre-servive and in-service activities. The two sets of distinctions do not overlap: many teachers begin work without teaching qualifications so that they may get initial training while they are working in-service. Then, in-service programmes may meet a variety of different needs, from initial training to updating or preparing teachers for new roles to helping reform the curriculum. Some of these purposes and distinctions are set out in Table—1.1.

The needs of primary education have dominated much discussion about teacher education and open and distance learning has been used more to prepare primary than secondary teachers. But this may be changing: earlier expansion of primary education is creating increased demands for secondary teachers, and in some cases to give primary teachers the skills to work at junior-secondary level. Basic education is increasingly seen as including both primary and at least the first cycle of secondary education.

Table—1.1 Purposes of in-service programmes

Purposes	*Sub-categories*
Initial training of unqualified teachers	programmes leading to certification short induction courses
Upgrading of teachers who already have a qualification	for sub-qualified teachers for qualified teachers
Preparing teachers for new roles	as head teachers to work in teachers' colleges
Training related to content of the school curriculum	for planned curriculum change refresher courses

Source: Based on Greenland 1983

Meanwhile teachers who move on to new roles, as head teachers or to work in teachers' colleges, often need and seldom get programmes of professional development to help them in their new job. A concern for their professional standing, long recognised by UNESCO as of major importance for the quality of education as well as for the condition of their lives, compels attention to programmes of this kind.

Who are the teachers?

Programmes of both initial teacher education and continuing professional development need to match the needs and circumstances of their audience. One size will not fit all. In particular, in designing a programme for teachers, we need to take account of:

- *their educational background:* This varies enormously between different countries and different levels of education. In some countries there are many teachers with little more than junior secondary education while in others all are graduates with a professional qualification as well. The balance between the different elements in teacher education is likely to affect the content of programmes for them.
- *gender:* It is difficult to recruit enough women teachers in many countries, enough men teachers in some. Programmes need to fit with the rest of teachers' lives and be sensitive to cultural norms and expectations that

affect their jobs. In some countries there are restrictions on women teachers' mobility that affect their ability to attend initial or updating courses.

- *their experience as teachers:* Again, the content of a programme for—say—unqualified teachers who have just left school may be very different from one for teachers with limited formal education but long experience as untrained teachers.

The teaching force is scattered so that there are logistical programmes to be overcome in providing in-service courses. If they have to travel to a central point, then there are actual costs involved for transport and possibly subsistence and opportunity costs for the time they are out of school. Family and other commitments may limit the ability of teachers to attend courses. There is obvious strength in any approach that can reach teachers without their leaving their schools for long journeys.

What is the curriculum?

The curriculum of teacher education is varied, and contested, is widely criticised, and in many countries is in a state of flux. In different countries emphasis has recently been placed on the importance of education to help countries compete in global markets, on social transformation, on technology, as well as on developing individual capacity. 'In different places we have got economics, social transformation, personal development, religion, technology, ethics, and a shift in the teacher's role, all among the aims of teacher education' (Perraton 2001: 2).

As a result, many education authorities are seeking fundamental changes in the curriculum. There is a widespread view that some emphasis, and resources, should shift from initial to continuing teacher education. At the same time, some authorities are beginning to revisit traditional and indigenous educational institutions in order to learn from their strengths and explore the possibility of integrating their work with a more modern curriculum. Demands on teachers continue to grow and become more diverse and their own education needs to reflect this.

Thus teacher education in many countries gives an impression of rethinking, and reconstructing of the curriculum. But it is not clear how far the rhetoric of reform has led to superficial or substantial restructuring. The evidence here suggests the former. A recurrent picture is the coexistence of traditional and newer curriculum models within one programme. This takes the form of two competing strands of thinking that, for convenience, can be labelled as traditional and progressive tendencies. The traditional is teacher-centred, based on behaviourist assumptions, has a transmission view of knowledge and regards the teacher as a technician; the progressive strand includes more active and participatory learning methods, is less authoritarian, places more demands on teachers and contains elements of constructivist thinking. The progressive agenda encourages the development of reflective practice among teachers. As a result, the traditional model of master-apprenticeship, of theory preceding practice, has become increasingly challenged and the coherence between education theory and the actual practice of teaching became an even more critical issue. Key questions then arise for the curriculum planner about the extent to which this agenda id appropriate for teachers who have themselves had only a limited background education. In a classic analysis of the realities of educational reform, Beeby (1966) warned against seeking over-rapid transformation and of the dangers of unrealistic expectations of teachers who were themselves teaching at the limit of their knowledge.

All of these issues affect the curriculum planner, regardless of the methods, timing or location of teacher education. If, then, we are planning to use open and distance learning for teachers we need to ask not only about how it can work—the theme of the rest of these guidelines—but also about curriculum policy. Critical questions are about:

- the balance between the four elements of the curriculum for the particular audience, taking account of teachers' own background education;
- the balance between pre-service and in-service education;
- the debates between traditional and progressive approaches and views about the appropriateness of defining teacher education in terms of a set of stated competencies;

- realistic expectations that will help the progress of curriculum reform but can be achieved with the support, interest and goodwill of teachers.

The planner then needs to consider methods that will fit both the aims of the curriculum and the circumstances of the learners. This in turn is likely to mean the use of a variety of different approaches—a theme we pick up in Chapter 3.

In the next chapter we look at the nature of open and distance learning, in order to assess how far it can meet their needs for teachers and for the educational services within which they work.

2

Is Distance Education Relevant?

To establish whether distance education can help with the teachers' demands set out in chapter 1 we need to ask what it is, whether it is legitimate, whether it works, and how much it costs.

What is distance education?

The language is confusing. 'Distance education' is sometimes taken to mean the use of television and at others the use of the internet. The words imply that students are always remote and never meet each other or their teachers. 'Open learning' suggests that anyone can enrol and start and finish when they line. 'New information technologies' sounds good but vague. These guidelines are about the use of a range of technologies in education, using a set of definitions that have general currency. Distance education has been defined as an educational process in which a significant proportion of the teaching is conducted by someone removed in space and/or time from the learner. Open learning, in turn, is an organised educational activity, based on the use of teaching materials, in which constraints on study are minimised in terms either of access, or of time and place, pace, method of study, or any combination of these. The term 'open and distance learning' is used as an umbrella term to cover educational approaches of this kind that reach teachers in their schools, provide learning resources for them, or enable them to qualify without attending college in person, or open up new opportunities for keeping up to date no matter where or when they want to study.

Open and distance learning often makes use of several different media. Students may learn through print, broadcasts, the internet and through occasional meetings with tutors and with other students.

Three illustrations take us beyond definitions.

The University of the South Pacific serves scattered audiences over the huge area it serves. It teaches education, and other disciplines, by combining correspondence lessons with broadcasts and with regular sessions at regional centres within its region. The university was one of the earliest users of communication satellites and is able to run two-way seminars with its students by means of satellite links. The university's early adoption of distance education has made good quality teacher education available that would have been beyond the resources of the individual small states of the Pacific.

In order to expand the supply of teachers as it came out of a period of civil war, Uganda has set up a number of programmes designed to equip untrained and unqualified teachers with professional skills. It has done this by combining teaching mainly through print with regular face-to-face sessions for student teachers and short periods of intensive study within conventional teachers' colleges.

The British Open University was set up in 1969 to widen access to education in Britain and has served as a model to many others. At the request of government it introduced a programme for a certificate in education for graduates who wanted to enter teaching but had no professional qualification. Teaching materials were distributed partly by mail and partly through the internet. Trainee teachers were based in schools where a mentor guided their teaching practice. Students used computer conferencing as an integral part of the course to interact with tutors and with each other.

Open and distance learning may use print, broadcasts, cassette recordings, computer-based materials, computer interaction, video conferencing, and face-to-face learning. We look at the choice of technologies in Chapter 5. The essence of it is that it enables students to learn without attending an institution. That has made it attractive for students who, for practical, economic, social and geographical reasons, cannot get to college. It also makes it particularly appropriate for audiences that are scattered, and audiences that cannot leave their jobs to attend full-time courses. The world's sixty million teachers are like that.

Is it legitimate?

Open and distance learning is often seen as barely legitimate. Its history is marked by the work of institutions that accepted student fees, gave them poor service, and kept their costs down by encouraging students to drop out once they had paid all their money. Learning at a distance, particularly from printed materials, lends itself to rote learning. If teaching material gives all the answers then there is no room for an individual response while if it fails to do so the student may feel challenged but frustrated. Distance learning can be a soulless and isolated activity so that dropping out is more attractive than going on. Most parents and probably most educational planners wouid encourage their own children to study at a conventional university rather than an open university. Few would argue that open and distance learning matches the best of conventional education as sometimes practised in rich universities in industrialised countries or in a golden age we think our grandparents might have been able to remember.

But there is a threefold case to be made for its legitimacy.

First, the evidence of public-sector open universities, and dual-mode universities that teach both conventionally and at a distance is that students can achieve examination results that match those of conventional universities. A significant proportion of students give up along the way and do not complete their courses. But this is true of all students working part-time and not a distinguishing mark of students learning at a distance.

Second, distance education has been powerfully effective in reaching audiences who could not meet their educational needs from conventional institutions. In Colombia, a radio-based school was, in the 1970s, reaching over 100,000 rural peasant students every year. The National Technological University in the United States is using satellite and broadcasting technology to meet the needs of engineers for post-graduate study without their having to leave their jobs and attend a campus. In China, the combined use of television, classroom sessions, and printed materials is providing university education to about a third of all the students in higher education. A church-based non-government organisation, the American private sector, and the government authorities in China have all perceived distance education as legitimate because of its power to widen access to education.

Third, where open and distance learning provides opportunities for student interaction with tutors, it allows open-ended dialogue, often regarded as the touchstone of legitimate education. Thus, while open and distance learning may lend itself to rote learning—as does learning in large classrooms—this is not an essential or defining characteristic.

The arguments are linked: open and distance learning is legitimate because it has a record of success in terms of the measures applied to conventional education but would be of little interest if it simply replicated for the same audience what could be done conventionally, and of little value if it got people through their examinations at the expense of more serious educational purposes.

Does it work?

The first part of that answer about legitimacy suggested that open and distance learning could work. But does it actually work for teachers? We can look at three kinds of answers—about student numbers, about outcomes in terms of examination results or learning gains, and about performance in the classroom.

The evidence on numbers enrolling on courses is solid and reassuring. Many programmes of teacher education, in all continents, have succeeded in enrolling students in significant numbers. We need, however, to go on to ask also about completion rates. Where teachers have been promised improved status or pay at the end of the course, completion numbers can be as impressive as enrolment numbers. It is programme to expand the teaching service in the 1970s, for example, Tanzania succeeded in recruiting 45,000 potential teachers of whom 38,000 went on to get their qualifications (Chale 1993: 31). In the case studies recently completed by UNESCO, completion rates varied widely. (The case studies are outlined in chapter 3, below). In Burkina Faso, very few head teachers dropped out. In the case of Nigeria, dropout rates varied from 27-39 per cent and the pass rates of those completing the programme varied from 55 per cent to 64 per cent. In the British Open University, completion rates appeared to be relatively high. In contrast, a programme in India had a completion rate of less than 20 per cent while about half the teachers learning about new communications technologies in Chile did not complete the course, partly because of difficulty in paying their fees. In both of these cases, in contrast with the Tanzanian example, students enrolled individually rather than being recruited in a national campaign and were not guaranteed promotion or a new status on completion.

There is evidence, too, that students on courses for teachers get reasonable examination results. A review of nine earlier case studies found that pass rates were between 50 and 90 per cent, figures that are probably in line with more recent data. It concluded that 'while examination success cannot be equated with teaching capacity, we can legitimately assume that a reasonable examination pass rate demonstrates that a programme was effective in teaching academic subjects' (Perraton 1993: 393). Rather than look at examination results, we might want to examine how well trainee teachers learned. Teacher education projects in Indonesia and Sri Lanka set out to measure learning gains and found reasonable evidence of effectiveness that is in line with the evidence on examination results (Nielsen and Tatto 1993).

It would also be interesting to ask whether the students of trained teachers performed better than those of untrained but unfortunately we have limited evidence, and hardly any of it from open and distance learning. A series of studies have yielded the disturbing results, from developing-country studies, that there was little difference in school outcomes with qualified or unqualified teachers (cf. Perraton 2000: 59-60, Avalos 1991, Torres 1996). One interpretation of this is that poorly qualified teachers are not much more effective than poor unqualified teachers and that there is therefore a case for improving—and spending more on—teacher education. Rich-country evidence bears this out. A recent study from the United States which compared student achievement and teacher policies within its states 'demonstrates that the states leading the nation in student achievement and those that have made the most significant gains in achievement are the states that have the most highly qualified teachers and that have made consistent investments in teachers' professional development' (Russell and McPherson 2001: 8). Better educated teachers probably teach better.

Only a handful of studies have followed trainee teachers into the classroom to see how well they are performing. This was, however, the subject of evaluations of distance-education programmes for teachers in Tanzania and Zimbabwe (Chale 1993, Chivore 1993, Mählck and Temu 1989). Evidence from these large-scale projects to expand teacher supply was reassuring: while direct comparison between students taught in different ways was problematic students' classroom practice stood up comparatively well (Parraton 1993: 394-5).

The available data are thin, partly for lack of good research, but for what they are worth are summarised in Table—2.1.

What does it cost?

There are three kinds of answers to this question. First, we can look at broad-brush comparisons between the actual costs of training cohorts of teachers through contrasting approaches. Second, we can look at the costs of different technologies; we come back to this in Chapter 5. Third, we can analyse the kinds of expenditure needed for teacher education in varying circumstances. We look at this below.

Using the first approach, a number of broad-based comparisons have been made between conventional and distance-education approaches in terms of the cost per student or cost per successful student. Of course these comparisons are crude, and lump together very different kinds of distance-education programme. But, for what it is worth, the evidence suggests that, above a threshold in numbers,

> with the relatively high comparison rates often achieved in teacher education, costs per successful student tend to compare favourably with those of conventional education. This differential holds true both for projects with quite modest costs per student, reflecting limited student support, as in Pakistan [as the Allama Iqbal Open

Table—2.1 Outcomes of some projects

Project, date, purpose	*Numbers*	*Outcomes*	*Costs*
In-service upgrading of unqualified primary school teachers, Botswana, Swaziland, Uganda 1967-78	Each in range 600 to 1,000	Successful completion rate 88-93 per cent Anecdotal evidence of impact on classroom performance.	n.a
Kenya programme for unqualified primary school teachers, to improve general educational background and achieve secondary examination passes 1967-73	8,433 over 7 years; annual enrolment 850 to 2,000	91 per cent passed examination and gained promotion. No firm evidence on classroom performance.	Cost per enrolment relatively high in comparison with alternatives.
Tanzania programme to recruit and train on the job primary school teachers for introduction of universal primary education 1976-84	45,534 in three annual cohorts	83 per cent qualified. Positive evidence on classroom performance. Weaknesses in science teaching and self-confidence among female teachers	Cost per successful trainee about half cost of residential course
Zimbabwe Integrated Teacher Education (ZINTEC) for secondary school leavers, trained on the job for expansion of primary schooling 1981-8	7,353 over four years	80 per cent pass rate. positive evidence of classroom performance but difficult to draw comparative conclusions	n/a
Nigeria National Teachers' Institute training primary school teachers TCII course after 2 years' secondary education 1984-90 NCE course after 5 years 1990	186,713 over period Enrolment of 14,909 on 1st cycle and 26,657 on 2nd cycle	Success rate thought to be in range 25 to 30 per cent of those entering; compares favourably with alternative; no evidence on classroom practice 21000 students graduated 1994	Cost probably lower than conventional college

(Contd...)

Project, date, purpose	*Numbers*	*Outcomes*	*Costs*
Pakistan Primary Teachers' Orientation Course (Allama Iqbal Open University) introducing new curriculum to primary school teachers 1976-86	83,658 total	56 per cent completed course; 38 per cent of original enrolment passed examination positive self-report on usefulness. No direct evidence of classroom effects.	AIOU graduate costs 45-70 per cent on conventional university costs
Indonesia Universitas Terbuka upgrading course for lower secondary teachers	c 5,000	Positive effects on subject mastery and in theory and practice in skills; relatively poor results in mathematics; apparent decline in attitudes towards teaching	Cost about 60 per cent of equivalent
Sri Lanka National Institute of Education training primary-school teachers with secondary level qualifications	c 5,000	Positive effects on subject matter and in theory and practice in skills; less successful than conventional college in mathematics	Cost one-sixth to one-third of alternative
Uganda Northern Integrated Teacher Education Project for primary school teachers 1993-95	3,128 enrolled	88 per cent completed and passed examination; some evidence of improved skills in teaching competencies	Cost per student about \$2,000 compared with \$2,500 in conventional college

Source: Perraton 2000: 80-1

> University Primary Teachers' Orientation, Course], and those with relatively high costs incurred for extensive student support and supervision of classroom practice, as in Tanzania [in its large teacher-education programme of 1976-84].
>
> *Perraton 2000: 128*

The figures are summarised in Table—2.2.

Interpretation of the figures takes us into the detail examined below in Tables—5.2 and 5.3 and to the third approach suggested above. We need to look at the differences in behaviour of the costs of conventional and distance approaches to teacher education. Open and distance learning is often characterised as having high fixed and low variable costs which therefore allow for economies of scale: with more students the unit costs go down. The large teacher-education programmes in China, or the early programme in Tanzania, demonstrate this. In considering teacher education, however, other factors are often as important in determining comparative costs. If trainee teachers study part-time, with reduced periods of residence at a college then there are likely to be savings in the cost of residence and governments are less likely to pay an allowance while they are studying. Furthermore, if trainees are teaching, either full or part-time, while they study, cost analysis needs to take account of the value of this work. (Total expenditure is lower if, say, untrained teachers study at a distance more than if they are taken out of the schools to attend a full-time course and a new cohort of teachers is put into the schools.) Costing needs to take account of arrangements for student support and, often critical, of arrangements for classroom teaching and its supervision (see Chapter 7). To examine the total set of differences between the two approaches we need therefore to examine:

- the scale of the programmes;
- the media or technologies used (see Chapter 5);
- the costs of face-to-face or residential study;
- the cost of other student support;
- the costs of teaching practice and of supervising or examining it; (see Chapter 7)
- policy on charging fees (see Chapter 6);
- the opportunity costs of taking teachers out of school for their own education.

Table—2.2 Costs and effects of some teacher-education projects

Currency: constant 1998 US$

Country, project, date	*Student number*	*Average cost*	*Educational and cost impact*
Tanzania TTD 1979-84	15,000 p.a. 45,000 total	1863 per student p.a. 7316 per graduate	Effects comparable to conventional education. Cost about half conversional education.
Brazil Logos II 1976-81	24,400	211 per student p.a. 741 per graduate	80 per cent pass rate. Costs lower than alternative
Sri Lanka 1984-8	c5000	116 per student p.a.	Cost 1/6–1/3 of alternative. More effective than alternative for some subjects but less effective for others.
Indonesia 1985-8	c5000	805 per student p.a.	Cost about 60 per cent of equivalent. More effective than alternative in languages but less in maths.
Nepal RETT basic teacher course 1978-80	3000	196 per student p.a.	Cost slightly lower than alternative; completion rate 83 per cent, pass rate 57 per cent
Nigeria National Teachers' Institute 1978-89	20,327	79 per student p.a.	Cost probably lower than regular colleges; completion rate estimated 42 per cent, pass rate estimated 27 per cent both rates higher than at regular colleges

(Contd...)

Country, project, date	*Student number*	*Average cost*	*Educational and cost impact*
Pakistan Primary Teacher Orientation course 1976-86	83,658 enrolled 31,674 completed	107-149 per successful completer	Cost per AIOU graduate 45-70 per cent of conventional university
Kenya in-service teacher training 1968-77	790	806 per subject equivalent p.a.	Cost relatively high; favourable effect on access
Kenya University of Nairobi B.Ed 1986-90	515	1096 per student p.a.	Cost thought to be lower than cost of residential equivalent
Nigeria COSIT University of Lagos 1980-8	2000	345 per full-time student equivalent 1304 per graduate	If opportunity costs are omitted then cost per graduate slightly lower than residential campus cost
Uganda NITEP project 1993-7	2750	2000 per successful student	Lower cost than equivalent

Source: Perratorn and Creed 2000.

Table—2.3 Comparison between the costs of conventional and distance education for teachers

	Conventional	*ODL*
Expenditure		
Residence	Likely to be a significant proportion of total costs	Cost likely to be reduced where students are in residence for smaller part of total study time
Grants, allowances	Often paid to full-time students	May be paid only for short periods of residence
Staffing	Staff time dominated by face-to-face teaching	Proportion of staff time required for materials development and for tutoring at a distance
Materials, media, communication		Costs likely to be higher and influenced by sophistication of media chosen; economies of scale are possible
Student support	Level of expenditure determined by amount of field supervision provided	Significant expenditure often needed for isolated students and to supervise classroom work
Annualised capital	Cost of teacher colleges and facilities likely to be a major capital item	Some capital required for distance education activities but these are counterbalanced by reductions in costs of college accommodation
Opportunity costs		
For students	Students may forgo national income by attending college	Teachers may forgo income from private tuition while studying
For ministry of education		If students teach while they study ministries avoid costs of funding their replacements
Income		
Student fees	Rarely charged	Are sometimes charged, especially where students are voluntarily upgrading their qualifications

Some of the differences between the two approaches are set out in Table—2.3.

Conclusions

The evidence shows that distance education, in its various forms, can work if well-designed can be educationally legitimate. It has been applied to the education of teachers and has been shown to be effective on a number of measures In terms of cost per student, distance-education programmes have often shown advantages over conventional programmes. With this kind of reassurance we go on, in Chapter 3, to look at the particular roles it has played in teacher education.

3

What Has It Been Used for?

Distance education has been used to teach, support and develop teachers for many years: UNESCO was a pioneer through its UNRWA/UNESCO Institute of Education which was training teachers for refugees forty years ago. Since then open and distance learning has been used in many countries of the world with a reasonable record of success. The use of new information and communication technologies has drawn new attention to open and distance learning and offers new possibilities. We begin by asking why it has been attractive to decision-makers.

Why use distance education?

The reasons are varied. It has been used to reach trainees in geographically challenging areas such as the riverine regions in Guyana, mountainous areas in Nepal, the dispersed communities of the Indonesian archipelago and the small island states in the Caribbean and Pacific. In some high population countries such as China and Pakistan, distance programmes have played an essential role in providing teacher education on a huge scale. In many Latin American countries distance education has been used widely to support curriculum reform and teacher upgrading. Teacher education by distance is being used to redress inequalities in teaching qualifications in post-colonial Namibia and Zimbabwe and in South Africa, as a tool for reconstruction of the teaching service in Uganda. In other countries, it is being used to reach marginalised communities such as refugees in Sudan, itinerant communities in Mongolia, and minority-groups in northern Pakistan.

Using distance education for teacher training has various potential advantages. Large programmes have brought economies of scale. In contrast to college-based training, distance programmes can provide access to courses on a much larger scale and wider geographical reach. It can overcome regional differences in access to teacher education. It provides a means of side-stepping the slowness and dilution of the cascade approach. In continuing professional development, distance education can help avoid the cost of replacing a teacher who has gone to full-time education. It can open up access to teacher-training opportunities for teachers with family responsibilities who are earning an income and need to remain within their communities. The establishment of a decentralised distance-education structure can also be used to support training in the districts and serve as a basis for the development of a programme for the continuing development of teachers. In print-poor countries, self-study materials can become a permanent resource. It can also 'put information about curricula and teaching approaches directly into the hands of individual teachers' (Robinson 1997: 125) and cut down the time between learning about new teaching practices and trying them out in the classroom. This is particularly important in curriculum reform and short professional development courses. Carefully balanced mixed-mode teaching can help to double and triple a college's training output per year. Where the infrastructure for them is in place, new information and communication technologies have opened up a range of new opportunities for course- and resource-based learning in teacher education.

Three general points need to be stressed.

First, distance education is of potential benefit to teachers because it can reach populations and can offer them education and training without their having to leave their schools. It has great logistical advantages. This means that if offers the chance of accelerating the supply, or the updating of teacher, beyond what could be done through conventional means.

Second, good programmes of open and distance learning have benefited from its strengths and avoided its weaknesses. Some aspects of teacher education need to be done face-to-face, or need close interaction with a tutor or with other students. Others do not. Programmes that combine conventional and distance methods are likely to be better than those that rely on a single approach.

Third, and for that reason, the more successful programmes have been carefully integrated into the structure of teacher education as a whole. They have not been designed as second-class alternatives to conventional education but as a part of a complementary system using a variety of different approaches, each chosen for its appropriateness to the curriculum and the audience.

Which parts of the curriculum is it good for?

We can go on to ask whether there are parts of the curriculum of teacher education for which open and distance learning is more or less appropriate. In Chapter 1 we distinguished between for elements of the teachers' curriculum: general education, subject knowledge, pedagogy, and practical teaching. All of these elements have been addressed in different programmes of distance education, using a variety of technologies, which are examined in more detail in Chapter 5. Distance education would seen to lend itself to the first element; there is wide experience of using open and distance learning methods for the traditional curriculum of secondary or tertiary education and a wealth of experience in offering an effective equivalent curriculum of this kind. In many countries there are teachers, or student teachers, with quite limited background education. Often these are the older and more remote teachers for whom open and distance learning may be a more convenient method of study than conventional education. Using open and distance learning to raise the level of their general education may be a simple and effective means of raising the quality of the teaching force.

Extending teachers' knowledge of the subjects they are to teach may be more demanding if it is asking teachers both to acquire new subject knowledge and at the same time to think about how they are to present it in the classroom. In Guyana, for example, a teacher training project dealt with this by running initial, pre-training programmes designed to increase the academic competence of unqualified primary and junior secondary teachers in English, mathematics and science in order to get them to the level needed for entry to a conventional teachers' college. Educators have also used distance-education approaches to bring new thinking and teaching practice about specific subjects of the curriculum. In Latin America regional collaborative projects have been set up in environmental education, mathematics and science. Some aspects of pedagogy or of child development lend themselves well to open and distance learning. Video examples of real-life classroom teaching in a variety of contexts can give teachers a wider range of exemplary approaches than would be possible in conventional face-to-face learning. Similarly the A-Plus television series in Brazil gives teachers regular access to access to examples of classroom teaching together with the voices of teachers talking about their experience and concerns.

As we saw, many programmes—properly—include elements of teaching practice and here it is generally necessary to combine what is done at a distance with arrangements for the supervision of classroom practice, the theme of Chapter 7 of the guidelines.

The general conclusion is that there are aspects of teacher education where the distant elements of open and distance learning are particularly appropriate, others that demand close contact with tutors or other students. We come back to the implications of this for planning and management Chapter 4.

How has open and distance learning been used?

In Chapter 1 we drew distinctions between programmes of initial education or training and those of continuing professional development, and between programmes for experienced and for inexperienced teachers. Initial teacher education and training is the programme of studies which leads to qualified teacher status according to the official standards of a country. It is the basic or first level of qualification for a teacher. It may be taken as a pre-service programme (before a trainee teacher begins work as a teacher) or an in-service programme (before a trainee teacher begins work as a teacher) or an in-service one (while an untrained teacher is working as a teacher). Continuing professional development enables teachers to extend existing knowledge and skills and develop new ones. Some of this takes the form of long structured courses leading to formal qualifications (diplomas or bachelor's or master's degrees). Other forms are shorter, concentrate on skills in managing children's learning or curriculum change and do not lead to additional qualifications. In some countries, qualified and unqualified teachers alike participate in continuing professional development. It may be provided as in-service activities (on-the-job learning) or out-of-school courses of varying length (off-the-job or in vacations).

In order to document recent international experience, UNESCO carried out a set of case studies on teacher education at a distance in 2001. The case studies fell into four groups which reflect differing uses of open and distance learning. They are summarised in Table—3.1, which distinguishes programmes for initial teacher education, for continuing professional development, to reorient teachers for curriculum reform and to support career development. Their main features are then described in box 3.1.

BOX 3.1: CASE STUDIES OF TEACHER EDUCATION AT A DISTANCE

Initial Qualifications

Nigeria: The National Teachers' Institute. The National Certificate in Education (NCE) is a print-based distance programme offered by the National Teachers' Institute in Nigeria, a unique distance-teaching teachers' college. It provides an alternative but equivalent route to minimum national initial teaching qualifications for working primary teachers in a country very short of qualified teachers and where conventional college output cannot meet demand. It aims to provide large-scale training in a high population country at affordable costs.

United Kingdom: Open University. The Open University's PACE programme uses ICT and distance education to support the school-based training of graduates in the United Kingdom. It reflects UK government policy to increase the role of school experience and the use of competency-based approaches in the initial preparation of teachers.

China: The China Television Teachers' College. The China Television Teachers' College (CTVTC), a part of the China Central Radio, and Television University (CCRTVU) since 1994, provides large-scale teacher education through a national distance teaching institution, distance education is included in China's strategic planning for teacher education and plays a significant role in initial teacher education and continuing professional development. Its aim is to provide large-scale teacher training at an affordable cost and to provide a unified system of teacher training.

Continuing professional development

Brazil: TV-FUTURA. A-Plus is a daily non-formal television series designed to stimulate interest in education, teaching and learning among teachers and other educators in the broader community. Taking a journalistic approach, it uses a private educational television channel to reach an audience of 13 million across Brazil. It also helps mobilise teachers into follow-up action through its Community Mobilisation Networks. These extension activities, aim to help teachers extend teaching practices in ways that include community involvement, participation and development.

India: Indira Gandhi National Open University. The Certificate in Child Guidance is a print-based distance programmes for primary teachers, parents and social workers, provided by the Indira Gandhi National Open University (IGNOU) in India. Using printed text, audio and video materials it provides a practically oriented, non-specialist programme which is not otherwise available. The numbers of students have been relatively small (less than a thousand per year).

Egypt: Cario University and Ministry of Education. Egypt has set up a national network of 39 distance-training centres in all governorates and, by using interactive TV technology, has provided scheduled short in-service courses training for teachers and also for educational inspectors, directors and leaders. Trainees in the centres are able to watch subject-specialist presenters in real-time and have the opportunity of putting questions to them via centre coordinators.

South Africa: University of South Africa (UNISA). The BPrimEd and BSecEd are print-based degree programmes in teacher education provided by the University of South Africa (UNISA), one of the world's largest distance teaching universities. Distance education plays a prominent role in teacher education in South Africa—more than a third of its primary and secondary teachers were involved in distance education in 1995. These programmes began as in-service ones for working teachers wanting to upgrade to degree level but later diversified to include a pre-service target group too, in response to government policy change.

Reorientation of teachers for curriculum reform and change

South Africa: Open Learning System Educational Trust (OLSET). English in Action is a South African interactive radio programme run by an ngo, with two audiences: primary school children and their teachers. Through a well-structured curriculum and active learning approaches, the children learn English while the teachers improve both tneir English and their teaching of it. This non-formal programme asks teachers, many of whom have low levels of English or poor teaching methods, to lead language development activities, such as games or pair work and to mediate content, if necessary, in the mother tongue.

Mongolia: UNICEF and the Ministry of Science, Education and Culture. An in-service programme for primary teachers in a transitional country with reduced resources for education and to support changes in curriculum content and teaching methods. Though new to the country, distance education was chosen as an affordable means of reaching more teachers more quickly more often than traditional provision, to reorient them to new teaching approaches and curricula.

Chile: Universidad de La Frontera. This in-service programme aims to teach teachers to learn to use information and communications technology (ICT) in their teaching. It uses ICT to teach teachers to use ICT. Distance education, through fairly new to Chile, was chosen in order to extend the geographical reach of the programme, otherwise available in a conventional face-to-face form, and to meet the teachers' needs for new skills and knowledge created by the recent widespread provision of computers to schools.

Career development

Burkina Faso: Ministry of Basic Education and Literacy and RESAFAD (the African Network for Education at a Distance). This was part of a multi-national programme for West African francophone countries aimed at increasing the management capacity of head teachers. The programme benefited from the use of new information and communication technologies to help the process of course development but used print, coupled with meetings of head teachers, to reach its scattered audience. The programme reached about a quarter of Burkina Faso's head teachers and there is some evidence from reports of school inspectors of more efficient school management as a consequence of the course.

These categories inevitably overlap: career development may, for example, be regarded as part of continuing professional development; some of the programmes have more than one audience, and may include qualified and unqualified teachers, teachers studying for initial qualifications and those using the same programmes to upgrade their qualifications. In general, distance-education programmes have been developed with varied

Table—3.1 The case studies

Category	*Cases*	*Technologies*
Initial qualifications	An alternative route to primary teacher qualifications, Nigeria.	Print with face-to-face meetings.
Programmes leading to qualified teacher status.	Using ICT to support school-based initial teacher education, United Kingdom	Print, computer communications, face-to face meetings, video and audio, written feedback on assignments.
	Reaching teachers through television, China	Television and video copies, some print, audio-cassettes, face-to-face classes or meetings.
Continuing professional development	Television-plus; journalism in the service of teacher development, Brazil	Television and video copies, magazines newsletters, telephone 'call-in' centre, fact-to-face meetings.
Programmes and activities, extending teachers' knowledge,	New routes to teacher education degrees, South Africa	Print with some face-to-face meetings, audio- and video-cassettes and some small optional element of computer communications
skills and expertise throughout a teacher's working life.	Developing primary teachers' knowledge and skills in child guidance, India	Print, face-to-face meetings and some audio- and video-cassettes.

(Contd…)

Category	*Cases*	*Technologies*
Reorientation of teachers for curriculum reform and change	Interactive radio for supporting teachers of English a second language, South Africa	Radio programmes, audio-cassettes copies, print and some face-to-face meetings.
	Reorienting primary teachers to new teaching approaches, Mongolia	Print and audio (radio and audio-cassettes). some videos and face-to-face meetings.
Supporting teachers in changing what they teach and how they teach it.	Teachers learning to use information technology, Chile	Computer communications for an online programme, for delivering materials, supporting interaction, providing access to databases and submitting coursework.
Teacher's career development	Professional development of head teachers in Burkina Faso	Print and face-to-face meetings.
Programmes to extend the careers of qualified teachers.		

intensions: of widening access to teaching qualifications; of disseminating good practice; of strengthening the education system as a whole by reaching not only teachers but the wider community; in enabling school-based training and professional development and as a means of strengthening the links between theory and practice, focusing on the school as a site of teachers' learning.

We look at each category of teacher education in turn.

How has it worked for initial qualifications?

First, some countries have used distance education to provide a route to initial qualifications for significant numbers of teachers, both new entrants to teaching and experienced unqualified teachers. The China Television Teachers' College and the National Teachers' Institute in Nigeria have long experience of this approach and both have become recognised and institutionalised parts of the regular education system in their countries. In a programme that reflects an official policy shift towards more school-based training, the Open University in Britain has run a school-based qualifying programme for graduates who want to enter teaching but have had no professional teacher training.

These three examples from very different countries illustrate differing roles for open and distance learning in initial teacher education. The programmes in China and Nigeria take in large numbers of entrants and make a substantial numerical contribution to increasing qualified teacher supply. The Open University programme makes an important contribution towards providing alternative opportunities for trainee teachers but, in comparison to the Nigerian and Chinese cases, its numerical impact on British teacher supply is modest. The 1998 figures reveal an intake of 1933 trainee teachers compared with a national annual intake of new teachers of some 30,000. However, there is some evidence that twice as many teachers who study at a distance through the Open University courses stay in the profession as the national average where up to 40 per cent of newly trained teachers in England leave teaching within three years of qualifying (Personal communication). This finding is consistent with data from teachers working in very different circumstances in Zimbabwe where over 90 per cent of teachers trained through the ZINTEC distance-education programme were reported to be still working in the schools six years after the programme ended (Perraton 2000: 67).

The three programmes provide initial training for different levels of learners, from secondary-level entry qualifications in China and Nigeria to graduate entry in the United Kingdom. The programmes also handle the management of teaching practice in different ways, reflecting the regulations and norms of the different countries and the importance placed on it within different teacher education systems. While the whole programme from the Open University is designed round school experience, in China this is given little emphasis. In the British programme, contact with students on teaching practice in schools and a reduction of their isolation—a problem area in all initial teacher education programmes—is facilitated by the employment of information and communication technologies. The labour-intensive nature of the management of school practice, together with the use of new technologies and of several other media in combination, is likely to increase the quality of teacher preparation but also to increase costs.

What is its role in continuing professional development?

Initial teacher education is no longer seen as enough. Distance education is therefore also being used to raise the skills, deepen the understanding and extend the knowledge of teachers. Some programmes are broadly focused while others are targeted at specialist groups. Programmes are taken either by individuals or by groups of teachers who are encouraged to participate by their schools or their employers. For example, a non-profit television station is taking the lead on supporting school groups in Brazil. In other cases, programmes are available for individual teachers who want to improve their skills and their status, often enrolling on an individual basis, and at their own expense. Indira Gandhi National Open University in India has a number of programmes of this kind. The University of South Africa also offers programmes on this basis. Their B.Ed. programmes are for experienced underqualified teachers and also new entrants to teaching, which serve to meet individual goals as well as contributing to the policy goal of a graduate teaching force. Some programmes are aimed at the upgrading of teachers' qualifications required by official policy on new national standards, as in China, for example.

In these and other examples planners have chosen to use open and distance learning techniques to meet the needs of their scattered audiences. In doing so they have been able to take practical moves to provide long-term benefits, in terms of their capacity and status, to individual teachers as well as the education systems within which they work. In both England and Pakistan, for example, ministries of education have called on national open universities to distribute information and training on new curricula, rather than attempt to bring teachers together for this purpose. Some programmes using mass media have also sought to widen the audience beyond the core target of teachers to the broader community. The A-Plus television programme in Brazil uses mass media on a large scale to reach a wide community of viewers while at the same time using the series as a launching pad for further activities by groups of teachers.

How can it help curriculum reform?

Distance education can have a role in programmes of curriculum reform which aim to change either the content or the process of education. In South Africa, the Open Learning Systems Educational Trust is using radio to improve the teaching of English, and to support teachers in this work. In Mongolia, radio and print are used across large distances to reorient teachers to official changes in curriculum and teaching methods within a country in transition. In response to policy initiatives aimed at establishing the use of information and communication technologies in schools, the Universidad de la Frontera in Chile is using the technologies to support teachers who are teaching these subjects.

The Universidad de la Frontera programme, supporting the teachers involved in the Enlaces project which introduced information and communication technologies to schools in Chile, provided an online programme for teachers, as an alternative option to face-to-face programmes and ensured that the course assignments were of an applied nature. Though the cost of the two alternatives (face-to-face and online) were about the same, the online programme appeared to achieve more change, in fostering more familiarity with the technologies and the development of a 'network communication culture' missing from the face-to-face version. The OLSET programme in South Africa has been effective in reaching large numbers of teachers not only with prescription and advice on how to teach English as a second language but with well-designed lessons, provision of models, guidance in using the radio or audio-cassette resources and support for changes in teaching methods. There is some evidence that not only has the programme reached large numbers at low cost, it has been effective in helping young pupils to improve their English and teachers improve their teaching as well as their English. Using radio in a different kind of way, as a typical magazine and involving teachers in topic identification and programme construction, primary teachers in Mongolia became familiar with new ideas about child-centred teaching and other new approaches and were able to apply them to their teaching.

Can it support teachers' career development?

Distance education has been used for teachers' career development. As they seek promotion, or aim for the next qualification level, or aspire to become a head teacher, or work in a teachers' college, or become an inspector, teachers need to acquire new skills. A multinational distance-education project in West Africa has developed a training programme in school management for head teachers and aspiring heads. In Burkina Faso, over a quarter of the country's head teachers (whose professional development is increasingly seen as a key element in school effectiveness) developed new knowledge and skills within four years. This served at least three functions; it furthered their careers, built capacity in the head teacher cohort and provided professional development. This experience, and the demand for specific training and support for head teachers in many other countries, suggests that this as an area of work that merits investment and expansion. It is the kind of programme that will enhance and strengthen the status of teachers.

Conclusion

Open and distance learning has been widely applied to teacher education and there is some record of success in its use for all four regular elements of the curriculum—general education, subject-specific knowledge, pedagogy, and practical teaching. With differing emphasis on different parts of the curriculum it has been deployed for teachers at different stages of their careers, and in support of national programmes of development and of curriculum reform. The record of achievement is solid enough both to have some confidence in its use and to draw some generalisations about how to plan and manage it, the theme of the following chapters.

4

How is It Planned And Managed?

To sum up the argument so far, open and distance learning has been applied to the problems of both the initial education of teachers and their continuing professional development, with some evidence of success. In this section we ask how programmes of this kind can be planned and managed before going on to ask about specific management decisions in the four key areas of technology, funding, classroom practice, and assessment.

The prime task of the planner or manager is to match educational purpose, administrative structure, and teaching methodology. This cannot be done in a vacuum. The history of distance education is littered with projects that looked good initially but could not be sustained as they were not built into national educational systems. Decisions about such issues as the allocation of government resources, the recognition of qualifications, or the use of teachers' college facilities or staff are all likely to have implications for the educational service as a whole. Some of the planning choices within open and distance learning will affect people outside a ministry of education: teachers' associations and unions will be interested in the conditions of service for teachers working in a new role; broadcasting agencies, asked to transmit broadcasting materials, will certainly have a view about the timing of broadcasts and may want a measure of influence or even control over their content.

Identifying the educational purpose is all-important. If the purpose and audience lend themselves to open and distance learning, then it makes sense to explore the non-conventional options open to the manager alongside the conventional approaches of teacher education. The point of these guidelines is not to argue for the application of open and distance learning to every problem in teacher education but to suggest where and how it can be used. The most successful programmes are those where open and distance learning is closely integrated with other approaches to education and professional development.

What is the policy framework?

The planning is open and distance learning may involve policy issues at international, national and institutional levels.

The international issues arise in part because the forces of globalisation are affecting the content and practices of education, in part because new policy issues arise when education is no longer confined within national frontiers. Programme planners are thus increasingly exposed to innovations in teacher education and need to make judgements about the desirability, feasibility and acceptability of these internationalised ideas within their country and programme. Changes to more practice-based teaching education, for example, have been encouraged internationally and become part of the common discourse about education. As we see in Chapter 7, this has major implications for the local planning, implementation and management of programmes for teachers. International conventions on the role and status of teachers as agents of change naturally affect national policy. At the same time, educational cooperation across borders, and cross-border enrolment, put on to the decision-makers' agenda jurisdictional questions about cross-cultural transference and language and about the control of cross-border enrolment and its accreditation or recognition.

At the national level, lines of responsibility for open and distance learning within government are likely to be complex and do not just lie with the education sector. Increasingly, the development of distance education raises questions that have to be answered within a national communication policy, part of which will be a policy for the educational use of communications. Political, economic, technical and regulatory issues may all need to be considered. Some of these issues concern the respective roles of the private and public sector; educational institutions are likely to seek access to telecommunications on favourable terms, possibly through the use of governments' regulatory powers in the telecommunications sector, or may want more freedom to use telecommunications than has traditionally been available. Other areas to be considered in a communications policy include:

- investment policy, in relation both to the public sector and to the encouragement of particular areas of private-sector investment;
- policy on tariffs and on any common carrier requirements;
- government purchasing policy, and policy for the use of communication technologies for government's internal communication;
- technical standards including frequency allocation, systems reliability;
- the national development of national capacity and expertise;
- scheduling, influence, control over content and intellectual property;
- issues of equity and access.

Within the education sector, decisions about such issues as the allocation of resources, fee policies, the recognition of qualifications, the regulating and monitoring systems needed or the use of teachers' college facilities of staff are all likely to have implications for the educational service as a whole. Questions need to be addressed about the most appropriate contribution open and distance learning can make to different levels and types of education, including primary, secondary and tertiary education, and technical and vocational education and training, as well as to teacher education. Questions are also likely to arise about the national or regional location of responsibility for distance education. Many planning decisions will affect people outside a ministry of education: teachers' associations and unions will for example, be interested in the conditions of service for teachers' working in a new role.

For institutions changing to dual-mode status, a key issue will be the balancing of resources allocated to open and distance learning against those of conventional provision and the systematic planning of policies to manage institutional change effectively. This is likely to include new faculty policies (new contractual and workload agreements, training renegotiation of union contracts, evaluation and support); student policy issues (material delivery, library access, counselling, financial aid, registration and record-keeping, technical support) and legal policy development (intellectual property including ownership of materials, copyright, and faculty, student and institutional liability).

What different elements do you need to make it work?

As we saw in Chapter 2, the use of open and distance learning forces us to distinguish between a number of different educational and administrative jobs that may be done by a single institution, even a single person, in conventional face-to-face education. In open and distance learning functions are divided between different sections of the same organisation, or between different organisations. Where a project or programme is to enrol, advise, teach and examine students it needs structures for a set of different functions. (Programmes that simply provide resources for teachers, whether through print or broadcasting or on the internet, as opposed to courses on which learners enrol, will need appropriate structures for making and distributing the resources but not the whole range of functions set out below.) To make distance education work you need structures and facilities for:

- governance, planning, management and funding
- materials development and production
- materials reproduction and distribution
- student recruitment and advice
- student support including the supervision of classroom practice
- assessment and evaluation of learners
- feedback system/formative evaluation
- record systems.

Any organisation needs a governance structure that will make major policy decisions; arrangements of planning, management and funding are likely to be the responsibility partly of people working within a distance-teaching institution and partly of people outside. The development of teaching materials—or their acquisition from outside—is a basic function: distance education depends on such materials. They may be developed in-house, or by external course writers, and are likely to be in a variety of media. An institution will need not only writers but people who can edit materials, so that they work effectively at a distance, and people to brief and train writers and editors. Materials than need to be reproduced, if they are in the form of print or cassettes or cd-roms and distributed. Broadcasting or video-conferencing also demand a distribution function of a different kind. Structures and systems are needed to recruit students and advise them about the programme. Most students need support, guidance, and feedback on their work. Where teacher-education programmes include a practical element, concerned with their competence or skills in the classroom, arrangements are also needed to supervise this. Then, in many programmes students need to be assessed and their work examined or evaluated. Finally, a feedback system on the work of the institution or programme as a whole is needed to provide checks on how well it is working while a record system, important for any form of education, is indispensable where students are dispersed, needs to be designed and maintained.

Each of these topics demands attention. There are many guides to them, some of them identified in the annex. We look in the following four chapters of the guidelines at the key areas for the purposes of teacher education of technology (which shapes decisions about materials development and support for students), funding classroom practice and assessment. The identification of these elements makes it possible to go on and look at the choice of models for managing them.

What models are there for managing it?

A variety of different structures or models have been used for teacher education at a distance and are set out in Table—4.1.

Table—4.1 Some models for organising teacher education

Model	*Example*	*Comments*
Ad hoc arrangement made by ministry of education	MITEP Uganda	While this makes it possible to deploy resources quickly it may not be a sustainable model
Single or dual mode teachers' college	NTI Nigeria Belize Teacher Training College	The Nigerian case is the only example of a specialised distance-teaching teachers' college
Single or dual-mode university	IGNOU UWI	Many universities with distance-teaching capacity have been asked by MOEs to run programmes for teachers
Multi-country programme	RESAFAD head teacher training University of the South Pacific	Can share international resources and be of particular value for small states
NGO single-purpose project	OLSET	Speed and vibrancy of ngo activity has to be balanced against problems of sustainability and of coherence with government activity
Consortia and partnerships	TV Futura Brazil	If problems of integration can be overcome, a partnership of this kind may, as in Brazil, bring together an ngo, a broadcasting station, schools and a private-sector publisher.

In some cases a ministry of education has set up a project directly, making *ad hoc* arrangements for all the necessary functions. This will the case, for example, in both Tanzania and Uganda, at different dates, in order to run an emergency programme to expand the number of teachers rapidly. While this had the merit of speed, and meeting immediate demands, it has not generally resulted in a sustainable system.

Then there are many examples in which prime responsibility rests with a teachers' college. Most often this has meant that a college, which is already teaching conventionally, acquires new responsibilities for teaching at a distance. The Belize Teacher Training College developed a new, part-time distance version of their conventional initial teacher-education programme, drawing on existing faculty members to develop distance materials but also to train new classroom supervisors and assignment markers at a district-level. Staff had to acquire the skills needed for these new roles. In Nigeria, uniquely, the National Teachers' Institute exists just for teacher education and teaches entirely through open and distance learning. The advantage of these approaches is that the colleges should already be familiar with the needs of teachers and potential teachers and may have an infrastructure for supervising teachers in the classroom. At the outset, however, a teachers' college which is beginning distance education needs to develop skills—in material development for example—that its staff do not already possess.

Universities have also been called on to play a role here. They may have two areas of expertise: in teacher education where they have a faculty of education and in open and distance learning. Using a university for teacher education makes it possible to take advantage of structures and systems that are already in place. There may, however, be problems of fit and adjustment if a university has no experience in, say, the education of primary-school teachers which has generally been the responsibility of non-university teachers' colleges. There have also often been practical difficulties within dual-mode universities in the almost indispensable job of developing materials. Staff tend to have competing pressures, too little time to write, and to be working in an environment where there is only a shallow pool of writers. The introduction of distance education can also be met with considerable resistance by faculty members since it implies a change in cultural practices. It can bring changes to workload and job security, may involve changed job descriptions and even a threat to a traditional autonomy over content; it may demand an unfamiliar approach to team work.

We can distinguish here between universities with both conventional and distance-teaching capacities and open universities which teach only at a distance. Dual-mode universities themselves vary. Distinctions can be drawn in terms of organisational integration or the capacity of a distance education centre. In some cases, for example, only a handful of courses are available through distance learning and administrative arrangements for open and distance learning affect only a minority of university staff. In contrast some mixed-mode institutions have integrated distance education in such a way that there is a breaking down of distinctions between on- and off-campus teaching. In some institutions, the capacity of a central distance-education unit may be purely administrative. In others, it has overall responsibility for the pedagogical quality of distance education materials, and for staff training. All of these variations in university practice will have a bearing on the skills that can be deployed by a university in a teacher-education programme.

Universities have run programmes of two kinds which, over-simplifying, can be described as supply-led and demand-led. In some instances ministries of education have turned to a university to run a national programme because it has the infrastructure for materials development and distribution. In other cases, a university has developed courses, especially for continuing professional development, because it is itself aware of a demand from teachers that will help their professional development. Indira Gandhi National Open University in India, for example, runs programmes on which students enrol individually, paying their own fees, in order to raise the level of their qualifications.

Three other kinds of models can be identified. There are examples of non-government organisations working on one aspect of teacher education, setting up their own structures either in parallel with or linked with the public education service. With external, donor, funding the Open Learning Systems Education

Trust (OLSET) in South Africa, for example, is offering training for teachers in the context of its radio programme for schools. Non-government organisations have played a particularly strong role in a region like Latin America where a pluralist tradition encourages them and assumes they can have a role in public education. There is also limited, but growing, experience of programmes that go across frontiers. The regional universities in the West Indies and the South Pacific have responsibilities in teacher education. The growth of telematics has promoted cross-country teacher education initiatives such as T3 in Europe and STAMP 2000+ in Southern Africa. The T3 project, a consortium of universities and other partners in seven European countries developed a European-wide agreement on the content and certification of information and communication technologies in schools. STAMP 2000+, initiated by the Commonwealth of Learning, is a co-operative programme designed to bring the benefits of distance education to the training and upgrading of unqualified upper primary and junior secondary teachers and administrators in eight southern African countries. In francophone Africa RESAFAD has been working on projects to develop resources that can be shared across frontiers. In most of these cases other than the regional universities, these projects have been concerned mainly with the development of materials rather than with the creation and management of a whole teaching system.

We look in the next section at the role of partnership of various kinds.

In choosing between the models it makes sense to begin by seeing what is available in the environment. If there is an existing open university, or a university with a distance-teaching department, it may make sense to use their infrastructure rather than creating something new. But this will not always be the case: a ministry of education may have such different priorities from a university that it makes more sense to create a separate structure. Sometimes, there are also advantages to bypassing the traditional system in an attempt to be free from its political or pedagogical constraints, or its inertia. Both OLSET and TV-FUTURA found that, by operating outside the state educational system, they were able to offer practically orientated teacher-led content that was not readily available through the state system. This benefit needs to be set against the risks, in terms of acceptability and sustainability, of operating outside, if alongside, the system.

The choice between options—or the development of a new combination of them—is likely to be a function of five issues: governance, funding, capacity and scale.

Questions of governance are about responsibility for and control of the various parts of the distance-teaching system. Who decides about which of the functions identified above? How are conflicts between any of the parties resolved?

The level and source of funding may be critical: donor funds, for example, may be available only to a government agency or, the reverse, only to an NGO.

If a project is for a limited purpose and for a short period then *ad hoc* arrangements may have a positive advantage. Tanzania, for example, was able to set up a teacher-education programme to expand its teaching force in a short time, calling on a wide range of national resources, in order to train an urgently needed 40,000 teachers. But it is often difficult to turn short-term arrangements into a permanent system and a one-off emergency solution to a problem may jeopardise the development of a sustainable structure.

Where an institution—whether an open university or an international agency like the Commonwealth of Learning—has existing capacity to undertake some distance-education functions, this may be a powerful argument for using them and setting up a programme in cooperation with them. In contrast, if a college is launching a new programme of distance education, as was the case with MIITEP in Malawi, it will be necessary to set up the necessary infrastructure to develop materials and teach students.

The scale of a programme, or of a country, may determine the model to be chosen. Small states in particular may need to rely on a regional or international institution because of the limited facilities within country. Teacher education at a distance has, as already noted, been a major interest of the University of the South Pacific since its establishment.

In considering the balance of advantages for any one model, and developing proposals that take account of those issues, the most useful touchstone may be to consider the links between the programme and the rest of teacher education. Unless these links are in place then an unorthodox programme has little chance of effectiveness or even of survival. In developing the links it is necessary, too, to keep in mind relationships between the centre and the periphery: from the student-teachers' point of view the centre may be the school in which they are working and the distance-teaching institution the periphery; from the ministry of education, both may look remote. From the planner's point of view the links between them are of paramount importance.

Can you have partnerships and how do they work?

In many cases, it will not be possible for any one institution to carry out all the functions needed for open and distance learning and they will be shared between several partners. An open university, for example, may be contracted by a ministry of education for the development and central management of a programme but this is likely also to involve coordination or cooperation with any national accrediting agency, with curriculum bodies and possibly with public or private-sector broadcasting organisations. Cooperation with local colleges of education may be necessary for the supervision and management of the practical side of teacher education. The National Teachers' Institute in Nigeria depends on educators from local higher education institutions to supervise and assess their trainees' practical teaching at least three times annually during the four-year course. The China TV Teachers' College provides core courses for its students but depends on Provisional Radio and Television Universities or other local educational institutions to supply learner support and local organisation, including the enrolment of students and management of the course. In practice, the whole organisation and balance of the course components is dependent on local conditions and can, therefore, vary considerably in quality. Mixed-mode delivery systems can involve a complex range of partners. The MIITEP programme run by the University of Malawi has a college-based and a distance-mode phase. During the college-based phase, teaching practice is assessed by teaching college tutors while in the distance phase, trainees are assessed by the host school's headmaster four times a week, regional supervisors (from local colleges) twice a term and college tutors five times during twenty months.

Partnerships tend to be fragile especially where different partners could, if they chose, replace each other. They are stronger if then functions are quite different, as for example, where one partner has a mechanism for developing material and another for accreditation but with no overlap between them. The idea of partnerships has been driven by three forces: the shift towards greater decentralisation, an increase in school-based teacher education and decisions to integrate distance education and conventional approaches. While the benefits, and sometimes the necessity, of partnerships one obvious, they represent management difficulties and

> as might be expected, have functioned with varying degrees of success. The complexity, time and cost of managing these crucial relationships with partners tend to be under-estimated at the outset, especially when several colleges and regional or district authorities are involved. Furthermore, consistency of quality is not easy to achieve in large geographically dispersed programmes with decentralised field operations, which also need to be responsive to local conditions. Problems in managing the system revolve around issues of responsibility, role definition, accountability, location of decision-making, communication and the control and co-ordination of part-time support staff.
>
> *Robinson, 1997: 126*

Programmes which appear to have been most successful at achieving effective articulation and channels of communication are those that are very systematic in their planning and spend time, ahead of implementation, in identifying needs, on the basis of consultation and among a wide range of stakeholders. This seems to be symptomatic of distance-education programmes and initiatives which have been freed from a pressing imperative of going to scale; which, instead, have recognised the importance of building up a consolidated base as a prerequisite for effective delivery. Key elements seem to include strong programme direction focused on strengthening co-ordination between partners, an internal research and feedback capacity and a concern to pay equal attention to the development of central and decentralised capacity. In India, for example, a district-based programme for the development of primary education has used open and distance learning alongside other methods of teacher education. It has combined strong decentralised decision-making and management with unequivocal support, if not direction, from the ministry. This support has opened up access to existing state-teacher education structures, resources and channels of communication at different national, state and local levels.

In some cases partnerships have gone beyond frontiers. In West Africa, for example, the programme to train head teachers in Burkina Faso was able to draw on resources from educators throughout the region. Teacher education in the Caribbean draws on regional resources through the University of the West Indies, which is owned by the governments of the region. In a recent development, teacher education in Dominica and Sri Lucia has been supported by a collaborative project with Canadian universities. External support and exchange (beyond funding that we look at in Chapter 6) may make it possible to:

- get information about similar activities elsewhere: international agencies including UNESCO and the World Bank publish information about open and distance learning while a number of information agencies have specialist interests in the area;
- share teaching materials with other institutions or acquire material from elsewhere: both the Commonwealth of Learning, in the Commonwealth and CIFFAD in francophonie have policies and programmes to encourage such sharing;
- get professional advice or consultancy on particular specialisms in open and distance learning; consultants have often been used in planning and development phases;
- seek specialist education and training: programmes in the practice of distance education have been provided to learners internationally by, for example, Indira Gandhi National Open University, Deakin University in Australia and the University of London, among others;
- enrol on courses internationally.

This last has got increasing international attention with the development of e-learning and the promise that internet-based teaching will share the world's educational resources and make distance education more widely available than ever before. Hype has reached beyond sensible hope. While there have been a handful of programmes that use the new technologies to deliver teaching across frontiers, as through the African Virtual University, for example, little of this material has been designed for teachers and much of it has amounted to the delivery of lectures over a long distance rather than the creation of an educational programme. As Chapter 5 explains there are serious limitations on the capacity of the internet to meet the needs of students internationally while the most demanding issues for the planner are often about student support and local classrooms, not about the development of impressive teaching materials or their delivery. Materials to support teachers are becoming available on the internet; both UNESCO and UNICEF, for example, have websites for this purpose.

In exploring the possibilities for international cooperation the planner will want to define the terms of the cooperation and is then likely to be guided by seeking a balance between the quality and economy that may be achieved by the use of external resources and the need for teacher education to match its national or local culture. In relation to teaching materials, for example, it may be possible to find high-quality materials developed elsewhere that promise good results in, say, mathematics. It is less likely that a course on classroom interactions, or relations between the home and the school, will easily travel across national or cultural boundaries. (Many educators lean towards the cautious here: while textbook publishers produce and distribute the same book to meet needs in half a continent, distance-education managers are more reluctant to use or adapt something produced even in a neighbouring territory.) Where whole teaching programmes are available across frontiers, these questions about cultural appropriateness and accompanied by issues about accreditation and recognition, and about local and national capacity building. As and when internet courses become more fully developed, educational planners will increasingly need to decide how far to recognise qualifications, obtained outside their jurisdiction, and how far their availability helps or constricts national development.

There are increasingly important regional developments in open and distance learning. The project in Burkina Faso is one example. Within the European Union, the European Commission has encouraged cooperation in all areas of education through open and distance learning and the use of the new technologies. In Southern Africa there is a long history of cooperation, including the cooperative development of teaching materials for distance education. From the planner's point of view, regional possibilities may look more fruitful than wider international cooperation, especially if there is a history of educational cooperation within the region.

Who does what in each of the models or partnerships?

Whether a teacher-education project is run essentially by a single organisation, or through a partnership between several of them, decisions are needed about the allocation of functions to different members of the partnership. In Table—4.2 we examine the location of the functions identified above in various different models and structures.

The seven programmes included in the table demonstrate the extent to which teacher education at a distance usually involves cooperation between partners. Perhaps the National Teachers' Institute in Nigeria has the greatest degree of autonomy in its work as a federal institution, with power to run its own examinations and award qualifications, and the capacity to work throughout Nigeria. But, not least because of the scale of the country, it needs to work with other institutions to provide the limit supervision it can undertake of teaching practice. Another institution with considerable autonomy, OLSET, has fewer links with other agencies than most in the table but a consequence of this is that it is not able to have the close contact with learners required for more formal courses. Nor is it involved in award of qualifications. At the opposite extreme, in terms of autonomy, is the District Primary Education Project in India which was designed both as a cooperation between a range of different institutions at federal, state and district levels and as one in which open and distance leaning was integrated with conventional teacher education.

The effective management of open and distance learning demands some central management of planning so that materials development, production and distribution one often run from the

Table—4.2 Distribution of major responsibilities within individual distance teacher education programmes

Location of responsibility 1	*Cetificate with School experience, Belize* 2	*MIITEP Programme, Malawi* 3	*PGCE, Open University, UK* 4
Governance, planning, management	Ministry of Education and Belize Teacher Training College (BTTC)	MoE	OU guided by Teacher Training Agency (TTA)
Funding	Government	Government	Government
Materials development and production	BTTC	University of Malawi	OU with BBC for broadcasts
Distribution: material reproduction and distribution	BTTC	6 Teacher Training Colleges	OU-BBC
Teacher trainee recruitment	BTTC	District Education Officers and TTCs	OU
Tutoring and counselling student support	District Education, Centres, BTTC, field supervisors	District tutors	School-based mentors and OU tutors.
Teaching practice supervision	District classroom teacher-supervisors	College-based phase: college tutors. Distance -mode phase: head teachers, regional supervisors and college tutors	School-based mentors
Assessment or accreditation assessment and evaluation of learners	Level 1: MoE Level 2: Joint Board of Teacher Education	Malawi National Examination Board	Certificate awarded by OU, Recognition as teaching qualification by TTA

(Contd...)

DEP-DPEPII IGNOU, India 5	*English in Action OLSET, South Africa* 6	*A-Plus, Brazil* 7	*National Teachers' Institute, Nigeria* 8
Collaboration of national, state and district agencies with management decentralised to district.	OLSET	Consortium of private -sector and ngo agencies	NTI
Government	Donor	Private sponsors	Government, student fees
Indira Gandhi National Open University (IGNOU) in collaboration	OLSET	TV-Futura with Community Mobilisation Network (CMN)	NTI
IGNOU collaboration	South African Broadcasting Corporation, community radiostations, OLSET	National educational channel and local re-broadcasting	NTI regional offices in 36 states
Shared between IGNOU, Delhi, IGNOU regional centres, District Institute of Education and Training (DIETs)	OLSET district coordinators	TV advertising and CMN	NTI regional offices
Local and district coordinators	OLSET district coordinators	CMN and school coordinators	NTI
School-based	Occasional by district programme supervisors	None	Limited, by staff of teachers' colleges
IGNOU	None	None	Accreditation: National Commission for Colleges of Education. Teaching practice externally moderated by mainstream teacher education colleges

centre; student recruitment and some student support may often rest there. Collaborative arrangements are most often needed for the supervision of classroom practice and for accreditation. The British Open University, for example, which has the capacity to undertake most of the functions, set up an extremely decentralised system for support of its certificate students, where mentoring became the responsibility of individual schools throughout the country. In both Belize and Malawi supervision of classroom practice was devolved from the centre to the staff of teachers' colleges. The two non-government programmes in Brazil and South Africa were not able to provide regular supervision. In these examples, responsibility for accreditation tends to rest partly or wholly away from the main distance-teaching agency. Even in the British example, where the university has the power to award degrees, and certificates and does so in this case, the recognition of the certificate, as something that gives the holder the status of a qualified teacher, rests outside the university. In Belize issues of accreditation take the institution outside national frontiers: responsibility for level one of the certificate rests with the ministry but for level two with the Joint Board for Teacher Education, based at the University of the West Indies, and responsible for teacher education outside Belize as well as within.

Two lessons emerge for the planner. First, it is often possible to find an agency with capacity in some areas of teacher education at a distance within the educational system. You do not therefore have to do everything on your own and, at the planning stage, it is worth exploring where different responsibilities can best lie. Second, collaboration tends to be difficult and demands links at various levels within the organisations for smooth running and the resolution of conflicts. The links may be particularly difficult to articulate in large, federal, countries where resources may be needed at federal, provincial and district levels. At the other extreme, open and distance learning may stretch the capacity of small states, with little experience in open and distance learning, and relatively few potential writers or tutors in any one institution.

There is, of course, no ideal or universal model for cooperation between agencies and the allocation of functions between them will be shaped by local needs and circumstances. What is common is the need to identify where the location of all the functions needed for effective distance education, to agree on shared or divided responsibilities where they fall to different parties, and to ensure that funding for the different elements is available and its distribution seen to be equitable. Transparency will buttress equity.

Who should do the planning?

The answer to this question depends on the organisational model chosen and the location of the initiative to use open and distance learning.

The main general principle is to involve all stakeholders. In most jurisdictions the support of a ministry of education is crucial for teacher education and it may also be necessary to consult with a teachers' service commission, if it has a role in the employment of teachers, and any accrediting agency. Teachers' associations and unions have a role to play both in planning and in considering the effects of teacher-education programmes on their members' conditions of service and opportunities for professional advancement.

Many programmes of distance education have made extensive use of external consultants. In some cases—though most often for the establishment of new open universities—international planning commissions have been established in order to bring together different national approaches. In others, consultants with a particular specialism have been brought in to advise on technical aspects of open and distance learning, often in materials production and in evaluation.

General advice is difficult other than to recommend using local resources, looking for a combination of people who each know about some aspect of what is to be done, and a strong degree of scepticism about advice from outsiders.

Planners' guidelines for choosing between the options

We can sum up the argument of this chapter briefly:

- Work within a policy framework that ensures your programme fits its national context and, where appropriate, its regional or international one. This may well involve looking at issues of communication policy as well as of educational policy.

- Identify the range of functions you need for your educational purpose and audience and make a dispassionate analysis of where these functions should be located and who should undertake them.
- Establish the strongest possible links between open and distance learning and conventional teacher education.
- Consult widely and ensure the support of stakeholders, establishing a system for continuing contact with them.
- Seek regional and international cooperation insofar as this fits with your aims.
- Consider what kind of partnership is necessary for your work and what strengths different agencies will bring to it.

5

What Technologies Can We Use?

We stressed in chapter 2 that a range of technologies is available and that open and distance learning is not limited to correspondence lessons—old-fashioned and boring as they sound—or to the internet—exciting but often unrealistic especially in many developing-country contexts. To choose between technologies we need to look at their strengths and weaknesses, to ask whether the infrastructure is in place to use them, and to examine the costs.

There is no single answer to the question 'which technology is best?' Indeed, one starting point for choosing technologies is to recognise that media do not differ in their effectiveness. Of course a particular subject, or a particular kind of learning, may lend itself to a particular medium; print is not ideal for learning the pronunciation of an unfamiliar language and following a radio programme is not the easiest way to learn how to strip a carburettor. But a long line of research, and much practical experience, has shown that where you can compare different media for teaching the same subject matter, there are no significant differences in teaching effectiveness between them (Clark 1983). Intuitive views about the superiority or inferiority of any one medium need to be treated with caution. There is experience of using radio for teaching mathematics, for example, while it has been seen as having advantages over television for some approaches to teaching art: you cannot see teachers' painting and copy it. The result is that we can choose our technologies on grounds such as their appropriateness, convenience and cost, reassured that many different combinations of technology are likely to be effective. There is some evidence to suggest that combinations of media are likely to be more effective than any single medium. Practicalities buttress this argument: if something is available both on the radio and in print then you have an alternative if you miss the radio programme or if the printed document does not arrive. A careful blend of media, drawing on their individual strengths and minimising then individual limitations, is likely to produce the best results.

What are the choices?

Within open and distance learning, technologies are used for two contrasting purposes: to distribute teaching material and to stimulate learning by means of one-way or two-way communication. An appropriate technology needs to be found to distribute material to students. In the case of physical teaching material, such as books or audio cassettes, material has to be carried direct to students or to a point from which they can collect it. It may be possible to use existing channels of communication with teachers for this purpose, or to rely on the post, or to set up a dedicated service. Broadcasting, by radio or television, video-conferencing and computer communication all offer means of delivering teaching material to learners without these physical arrangements.

Teaching involves more than distribution. Well-designed printed materials, cassettes, or broadcasts are usually designed to promote learning, often by stimulating an active response from the learner. In choosing technologies, therefore, the policy-maker has to consider not just how materials will be distributed but how they can be designed to facilitate learning and to resolve tensions between these two aims. Television, for example, may look the best medium for showing a simulation in engineering but is inappropriate if the only available television hours are at an inconvenient time or on a channel which does not reach most of the learners.

If open and distance learning is to involve more than providing resources to teachers, it also demands two-way communication.

This may be immediate, in the case of telephone tutoring of video-conferencing with a two-way audio circuit, or delayed typically through the use of written assignments. New technologies are reducing the lengths of the delays here: it is sometimes possible for learners to send assignments to a tutor by fax or e-mail. Two-way communication is also possible, of course, through face-to-face contact. In making decisions about technologies we need to consider not just those that are mediated but also the role of face-to-face contact if this is part of the distance-education system we are creating. Thus, the planner's decisions are usually about a set of technologies, chosen according to their appropriateness for the subject matter and the audience, and to their cost. The Open University certificate programme, for example, used printed material as the main means of presentation of the subject matter and distributed this partly through the mail and partly by internet. It was a specialist course, aiming at a much smaller audience than a foundation-degree course, and was not therefore able to use a large amount of television. It used a combination of face-to-face sessions and computer conferencing for dialogue.

A classroom teacher, writing on a blackboard, and getting questions from students does all three at once. In open and distance learning we may use print to present material, the mail to distribute it, and face-to-face tutorial sessions for feedback and dialogue.

Planners are likely to be able to choose between some or all of these technologies.

- Print remains the staple of much open and distance learning, providing a permanent document that is convenient to use. Distribution may be physical or electronic. Print allows two-way communication but only with a delay.
- Radio has been widely used for formal and informal teaching, helping to bring teaching alive, and overcoming the problems of physical distribution that may limit print.
- Television has obvious merits but tends to have costs ten times those of radio.

- Cassettes have been used for similar purposes to radio, overcoming the problems of timing that limit the use of broadcast radio.
- Video-conferencing allows specialists at a centre to reach scattered audiences provided they have the equipment to take part. Many video-conference systems allow for one-way video and two-way audio so that, for some of the audience, it becomes a two-way medium.
- A variety of computer-based technologies has been used including the distribution of sample lesson plans on cd-roms, setting up exchanges by computer conference between teachers' colleges, encouraging the interactive use of computer-based learning materials, encouraging the use of web-based materials, and using computer conferencing to encourage discussion among learners.

In making choices the planner is likely to be influenced above all by the convenience of the learner, the cost, and the need for a culture of maintenance. It will be necessary to maintain hardware and software: physical equipment needs maintenance and access to specialist staff and supplies. Software will need updating and improving on a regular basis. Unfortunately many programmes have neglected the importance of maintenance or of budgeting for it, referred to in Chapter 6.

In Table—5.1 we expand on this brief summary identifying the strengths and weaknesses of a range of technologies for teacher education.

What about the new information and communication technologies?

While open and distance learning does not demand that we use the new, computer-based, technologies, they present enough opportunities for us to consider them separately. The development of computer links is beginning to blur the distinction drawn above between distribution and teaching. It is possible, through an internet connection, both to distribute material to learners electronically rather than physically and to teach them, by means of a computer programme, or engage in dialogue with them by e-mail or computer conferencing.

Table—5.1 Media and technology uses in teacher education

Function in teacher education and development	*Strengths*	*Limitations and requirements*
Print		
Provides information, concepts and examples in a structured way.	A learning resource in a permanent form, permitting individual or group use.	Physical distribution of the materials can be slow or difficult in some contexts.
Can teach academic subject content, education theory and knowledge about pedagogy.	A protable and convenient resource. Copies can be used by more than one teacher.	Fixed content, not quickly responsive to sudden changes in school curricula or educational legislation or teacher education curricula.
Can link subject knowledge to school curricula and teaching methods.	Good for explaining theory and concepts and providing detailed information.	Requires relatively lengthy preparation time and team-working by those producing the materials.
Can combine expert input with teacher-produced materials. Can show teachers'	Can include a variety of source materials. Can be low cost but scale affects costs.	Cannot show teaching-learning interaction at work in real time in classrooms.
lesson plans, extracts from teachers' diaries and accounts, diagrams of class-room or equipment layout and examples of pupils' work.	Provides a common standardised resource. If well designed, can combine effectively with other media.	As a standardised resource, it may not meet the needs of minority groups or languages, or regional variation.
Can provide transcripts of teacher-pupil interaction for analysis. Can provide guides to action for teachers (e.g. in implementing new curricula or doing action research)	Can play a variety of roles, from lead medium to supplementary resource.	A one-way medium. Interaction is possible with the material, with the school environment applying ideas from the materials, with other teachers in local groups or with tutors.

(Contd...)

Function in teacher education and development	*Strengths*	*Limitations and requirements*
Radio		
Provides topical information and current news for teachers. Illustrates text content or addresses educational issues in a lively way, using authentic voices and varied sources (teachers, policy-makers, parents, curriculum developers, education experts). Can raise awareness about education in a wider community audience. Offers a forum for teacher exchanges (teachers' voices). Can reach all or most teachers at the same time to support faster and more widespread information dissemination.	Often widely accessible by teachers, Can be responsive to teachers' needs within a short time-scale. Provides immediacy in the materials. Can be very low cost per teacher. Equipment for production can be simple, relatively inexpensive and durable. Use of local radio can increase the relevance of programmes and respond to local needs or languages. Programmes can take a variety of formats and fulfil different purposes: a flexible medium. Can integrate effectively with print.	Ephemeral or impermanent, content lost unless recorded. Scheduled transmission times may be inconvenient. Has a poor and unglamorous image. Needs teamwork and collaboration. when integrated with other media (can be difficult to achieve in practice). Often limited by regulatory framework for broadcasting or lack of enabling policy for educational use. Commercialisation of radio increasing costs for production or transmission. Weak in conveying detailed or conceptually dense material. One-way medium.

(Contd...)

Function in teacher education and development	*Strengths*	*Limitations and requirements*
Interactive Radio		
Provides well-structured lessons for teachers and pupils alike in a range of subjects. Compensates for weak teacher-knowledge and can improve it at the same time.	Has proved effective in several contexts for teaching English as a second language, maths and other subjects. Can reach a mass audience at relatively low cost per learner. Can support teachers in subject knowledge and in demonstrating new teaching methods. Structures active learning as part of the lesson Can provide models of lessons	Scheduling may be at inappropriate times. Depends on regular and reliable transmission facilities and broadcasting infrastructure. Cassette tapes can substitute but lose immediately and need physical distribution. Needs skilled programme designers and structures for teacher support with training for them where interactive radio is new. A one-way medium. Interaction is with materials, with and between children in class and ideally with other teachers.

(Contd...)

Function in teacher education and development	*Strengths*	*Limitations and requirements*
Audio-Cassette Tapes		
Provides illustrations through sound. Can give examples of concepts and theory. Can convey information. Can provide discussion in a more natural way than through text. Can provide detailed instructions (e.g. in using a computer or manipulating equipment). Can provide sequences of conversation for close analysis. Can be used as a teachers' talking newsletter'. Can provide models of pronunciation. Can act as a 'voice in the ear', to guide teachers through processes (e.g. learning to use a computer or observation tasks)	Offers a permanent resource for individuals or groups. Is relatively portable. Cassette players are often widely accessible by teachers Can be re-played, stopped and started at will by learner. Combines effectively with print, and can extend the use of radio programmers through recording for re-play. Is low cost to develop and duplicate. Can be a more intimate or motivating medium than print if not, presented as a single-voice long lecture. Provides good models in language learning and teaching, and sequences of natural conversation. Can demonstrate communicative approaches in language teaching. Teachers can contribute to tapes or make them. Can be used by tutors to give feedback to students.	Audio-cassettes can deteriorate over time. Sound quality can be poor if a chain of recordings is made or if the equipment is poor. Cassettes need good management (e.g. accurate labelling, storing, mechanisms for circulating among teachers). Can fail to stimulate active learning if used just to deliver lectures. Tape-editing time often underestimated. Needs skilled integration with print or other media. Content often needs designing differently from radio programmes. A one-way medium.

(Contd...)

Function in teacher education and development	*Strengths*	*Limitations and requirements*
CD-ROM (Compact Disk-Read only Memory)		
Provides access to information for teachers in text, graphics, audio and video form. Can provide information on curricula content and teaching methods.	Can store large amounts of information on one disk. Relatively cheap and simple to copy and distribute. Provides random access to content, so a particular segment can be located without having to rewind as in audio-cassettes. Can substitute for lack of access to databases where computers lack connection to Internet.	Requires a computer with CD-ROM drive and software to access to disk. Stores less audio material than audio-cassette tapes. More expensive than audio-tapes. Making CD-ROM interactive increases development costs.

(Contd...)

Function in teacher education and development	*Strengths*	*Limitations and requirements*
Television		
Can reach a mass audience of teachers and the community. Can raise awareness in the community at large about educational issues and teaching. Shows processes in real-time or slowed down or in close-up (e.g. classroom interaction, language development, mathematical operations). Shows a variety of school and classroom contexts and teachers in action which teachers would not otherwise see, given the isolated nature of teachers' work. Gives teachers comparisons and bench-marks. Can show specialists or experts at work. Provides material as the basis of group discussion.	Can demonstrate real contexts and provide rich visual content. Can capture classroom realities. Can combine a variety of content (e.g. site visits to schools; interviews, dynamic simulations, and examples of teachers' work). Can be combined with other media. Can provide topical content.	High programme development costs and may be high transmission costs. But modest cost per viewer possible on large enough scale. Not always accessible to all teachers. Inadequate technical support at local level sometimes leaves non-functioning equipment. Often inappropriate transmission times for teachers. Sometimes replicates traditional lecture formats which fail to make effective use of the medium's capabilities. One-way medium. May foster passive viewing. Filming in schools requires considerable specialist skills and resources. Filming in studio classrooms is often easier but can lack authenticity.

(Contd…)

Function in teacher education and development	*Strengths*	*Limitations and requirements*
Video-cassettes		
Shows processes in real-time or slowed down. Shows a variety of school and classroom contexts and teachers at work which the viewing teachers would not otherwise see. Can provide separate segments for close analysis relating to different parts of the course materials, not only long sequence. Commercially-produced video-cassettes, for example, on child development or other educational topics, can be 're-purposed' for particular educational uses (segments selected and printed guides produced in relation to them).	Can be relatively low cost, depending on development costs and scale of use. Has some of the strengths of television but can be used in different ways for learning (under the control of the learner who can stop, start and re-play sequences). Can provide material for close observation and analysis, if teacher is guided either on the cassette or in print. Can be used by individual teachers or groups. Can be combined with print. Is a permanent resource. It can support active learning with good instructional design; demonstrate teachers' beliefs and practices; stimulate discussion; show the realities of teaching in different schools and compensate for teachers' lack of access to other schools; show simulations and role play (e.g. in head teacher training) or children's work.	Requires physical distribution of video-cassettes and access to playback facilities. convenient for teachers. Quality (picture and sound) can deteriorate if copies of copies are made, rather than from the master tape. The cassettes need good management (accurate labelling, storing, mechanisms for circulation). Then role needs to be carefully designed to embed them in the course materials or in relation to active learning, if they are not to be a marginal resource. Video may be poor technical quality (poor lighting and sound, one camera recording only the teacher (not the children) and poor educational quality (e.g. presentation of whole 45-minute lesson). Editing time is often underestimated. Needs professional makers to achieve good quality.

(Contd...)

Function in teacher education and development	Strengths	Limitations and requirements
Video use in Micro-Teaching		
Provides a means for student-teachers to observe themselves on recorded video in a teaching situation or simulation, and to get feedback on their performance through viewing the video and discussion with tutor and peers. Provides student-teachers with an opportunity for observing, interpreting and discussing the video material. Provides opportunities for observing and comparing the performance of self with others.	Is effective up to a point, in assisting student-teachers to appraise their own and others' performance and assist the initiation of reflective practice. Provides opportunities for practice and experiment followed by feedback helps the student-teacher develop specific skills (such as questioning, explaining, managing time-on-task, setting up group-work, using a particular teaching method). A short amount of recording can generate a large amount of discussion and analysis (5-10 minutes of recording can generate at least an hour of analysis and feedback) with a skilled tutor. Gives attention to the individual student-teacher.	Is labour-intensive and small scale, therefore relatively high cost as a form of face-to-face teaching. Effectiveness depends on the quality of the tutor or facilitator, the preparation by tutor and student-teacher, the tutor's skill in facilitation and timing of feedback. Has been criticised as concentrating on isolated, decontextualised and specific teaching skills or competences rather than deep understanding. Requires a room to be set up appropriately as a classroom, with adequate lighting and equipment but can be relatively low-cost to set up. More difficult to do over a distance.

(Contd...)

Function in teacher education and development	*Strengths*	*Limitations and requirements*
Audio Tele-Conferencing		
Enables real-time interaction among teachers and educators in different locations. Can bring together teachers, curriculum developers, specialists and policy makers in one event. Can be used for presentations and teaching sessions, discussions, course delivery (in combination with other media) and student support.	Can support development of teachers across large distances, enabling contact between groups. Is relatively easy to use (no large amount of technical know-how to master). Can be cost effective but depends on context and comparisons with alternatives. Can provide topical content at short notice more easily than print (has the immediacy (or more) of radio). Can be combined with video-conferencing (one-day video, two-way audio) to reduce video-conferencing costs and to provide interactivity where the infrastructure or budget does not support two-way video-conferencing.	Facilitating group discussion across a number of sites needs high levels of skills and preparation. Requires advance organisation, scheduling and coordination to make the event successful. Special equipment needed so that learners usually have to travel to venue. Costs vary in different countries, but can be cost effective when compared with alternatives. Requires adequate telecommunications infrastructure to function and ensure adequate sound quality. Requires additional materials or two-way graphics for some topics and subjects.

(Contd...)

Function in teacher education and development	Strengths	Limitations and requirements
Video-Conferencing		
Enables real-time interaction among teachers and educators in different locations. Can bring together teachers, curriculum developers, specialists and policy-makers in one event. Can be used for presentations and teaching sessions, discussions, course delivery (in combination with other media) and student support. Can show a variety of visual materials to participants.	Can support development of teachers across large distances, enabling contact between groups. Can provide topical content at short notice more easily than print (has the immediacy (or more) of radio). Can make scarce expertise available widely.	Has high start-up costs; usage levels need to be high enough to recover them. Requires technical support, including at remote sites. Requires students to travel to venue; given the cost of equipping sites, these are likely to be less local than options using different technologies. Where teacher interaction is possible at the local or district level, video-conferencing is likely to be a more expensive option. Where teachers travel long distances to in-service events, the video-conferencing option may be more cost-effective. The added costs of the visual dimension may not provide matching benefits over audio-alone.
Computers		
Provides access to information on CD-rom and local databases. A means of preparing materials for teaching if consumables are available (e.g. cartridges, paper). Provides computer-based learning materials for teachers and pupils.	Can provide access to large amounts of resources for teachers to select from and use as appropriate in their own contexts or for their own development. Its use helps teachers to develop their own personal computer skills.	The quality of software or learning programmes is sometimes poor. Technical support is needed and may be scarce in rural areas. Access is sometimes restricted for teachers. Training for teachers may be too little, and too narrowly focused on using the computer rather than using it for teaching and learning across the curriculum.

(Contd...)

Function in teacher education and development	Strengths	Limitations and requirements
Computer Communication		
Enables teachers to participate in larger professional communities, beyond their local ones. Provides access to databases, either on a local area network provided by the education authorities, or the Internet. Enables teachers to follow professional development programmes provided by remote institutions.	Can provide a wide range of multi-media materials, if the infrastructure (and bandwidth) permit. Supports a range of interaction, from formal to informal of varying group size. Can archive discussions for later use by other teachers. Allows teachers to participate widely and to exchange experience and materials in peer groups. Provides access to more sources of information and assistance, on topics from the specific ('How do I teach the new curriculum on environmental studies to Grade 3 children?) to more general educational topics.	Problems of access and cost in some countries. Requires an adequate infrastructure (electricity, telecommunications), affordable prices, supportive policy framework and investment of resources. Requires a change in perceptions and practices in teaching and learning (in contrast to common perception that having computer communications will of itself improving the quality of teaching and learning). If lengthy print materials are produced through downloading, this may increase costs per copy over those of centralised print production and shift costs to the teacher, school or district. Requires training for effective use (often neglected). Requires considerable technical support

New communication technologies are being used with four different functions in teacher education, over and above their use as tools for the writing and production of teaching material. The first is simply to distribute teaching materials; from the educator's point of view it may make little difference if materials are distributed by post or by the internet, though the implications in terms of cost and convenience for the user may be very different. Second, in some cases electronic communications allow simulated two-way communication. This is the case where a trainee teacher interacts with a computer programme instead of with a tutor; much early computer-based learning followed this model but it has been relatively unimportant for teacher education. Third, where computers are networked, or students have access to the internet, then computer-based technologies can be used for two-way or multy-way communication. Fourth, there is increasing diversification into resource-based, self-access teacher education in a variety of media. A range of dedicated websites has been created for the professional development of teachers. Wherever teachers have access to the internet, these sites can increase the exchange of materials and interaction between teachers and direct them to other teacher education resources, experts and professional associations.

Within teacher education, the new technologies have been used for two different purposes. One is training teachers to learn about information and communication technologies and their use in teaching as computers are introduced to schools. In many countries this is being done through face-to-face training programmes, often as part of initial teacher education. Some countries (such as the United Kingdom and Singapore) have developed policies which require all initial teacher education programmes to include compulsory courses in the technologies as a strategy for building capacity in relation to them. In other countries, no policy yet exists and teaching teachers about information and communication technologies is at best an option within teacher-education programmes.

The other role of information and communication technologies is as a means of providing teacher education, either as a core or main component of a programme or playing a supplementary role within it. In Costa Rica, for example, the ministry of education developed the use of the Logo computer programme within schools as part of a programme of curriculum reform. Teachers' colleges are beginning to experiment with the use of computer-based material to strengthen and broaden their curriculum. Both UNICEF and UNESCO are developing work of this kind.

While there is limited documented experience on the effectiveness of the new technologies for teacher education, the available evidence suggests that we can propose three lessons for planners, mainly about capacity building.

- First, the development of teachers' capacity in using the technologies cannot happen in isolation. Plans need to take account of the use of the technologies elsewhere in the education system and in the wider environment. The technologies necessitate an appropriate technical infrastructure and funding to support it.
- Second, if the use of the technologies is seen as a function of teachers generally, this needs to be reflected in national policies and strategies and in the curriculum for both initial teacher education and continuing professional development.
- Third, while teacher educators are a key element in establishing the use of information and communication technologies in education, many teacher educators themselves lack skills and training in the use of the technologies or opportunities to apply and develop their knowledge and skills.

What are the prerequisites for each of them?

In choosing technologies we need to think both about their educational strengths and weaknesses, summarised in Table—5.2 and about the prerequisites for their production, reproduction, distribution and use. If, for example, we want to consider using radio we need to ask who will produce the programmes, how they will be broadcast (by a local or national broadcaster, on what frequency and at what time, and at whose cost), and about their reception, exploring whether learners have access to radio and either mains electricity or an affordable supply of batteries. It is important to ask questions about prerequisites both at the centre and at the periphery: it is not enough to produce good materials if they cannot be distributed or, for lack of access or shortage of particular technical equipment, learners cannot use them. In Burkina Faso, for example, as one of the least developed countries with a scattered population, the infrastructure in place meant that it would be unrealistic to use any medium other than print for teacher education.

The scale, and organisational location, of the project or programme is likely to shape the answers to these questions. OLSET in South Africa has used radio for schools, at a modest cost per learner, because it is a relatively large country using broadcasts in a single country, and with a national infrastructure that means many schools can use radio. In contrast, computer-based learning would not be realistic for its many rural schools. In Brazil and China the scale of teacher education is so big that it is possible for educators to have access to television through a non-government-private sector consortium in one case and a state-backed university in the other.

What do they Cost?

In examining costs, we need to distinguish between total cost and cost per student or cost per successful student: as noted above, it is possible to justify the relatively high costs of a medium like television where student numbers are high enough to bring down the unit cost. Then, in examining each medium or technology, it is useful to ask three sets of questions. First, we need to distinguish between the cost of setting up or initiating work in a particular medium from its running costs. Next, we need to consider how far the running costs are fixed or vary, usually with the number of students. And, third, it is useful to distinguish between the costs of producing teaching material, the costs of reproduction, of distribution and of reception. At each stage the planner is likely to have another practical question: who pays. For some of the costs may fall on the institution, some on national, regional or local government, and some on the individual student. In Table—5.2 we summarise the nature and location of costs for various media, looking at the same time at their possible use for one-way or for two-way communication.

Table—5.2 Nature and location of some costs

Medium	Features	Location of expenditure		
		Reproduction	*Distribution*	*Reception*
Print	Initiation costs can be modest Organisation costs fixed; reproduction costs vary with number of copies Level of costs differ widely according to quality of print Can be two-way if assignments included	Institution	Institution	Institution
Television	Initial installation cost high Production costs fixed Distribution costs fixed for given transmitter coverage Unit cost is likely to be high below 200,000 students then to rise again above 1 million One-way	n/a	Institution but may be shared with broad-casting agency	Local institution for group study or student if individual to provide set
Radio Audio/video cassettes	Installation cost relatively high Production costs fixed Distribution costs fixed for given transmitter coverage Costs generally one tenth that of tv One-way	n/a	Institution but may be shared with broad-casting agency	Student (e.g. batteries)

(Contd...)

Medium	*Features*	*Location of expenditure*		
		Reproduction	*Distribution*	*Reception*
Video-conferencing	Significant installation costs at centre and at each location Production costs may be low and are fixed Distribution costs depend on means of transmission May be two-way if audio feedback link is included	n/a	Institution	Institution
Production of computer-based teaching material	Some initiation costs Production cost likely to be very much higher than for print Distribution costs dependent on choice between cd-rom and internet distribution	Institution if cd-rom	institution if cd-rom	Learner
Computer conferencing	No production cost. Distribution costs dependent on cost of access to telephone network Running costs for institution vary with number of students Multi-way	n/a	Institution/ Student	Learner

The actual costs of a particular technology will depend on local circumstances and it is not possible to set out an international set of standard prices. Even within a single medium or technology costs can vary widely: sophisticated television documentaries have far higher production costs than teaching programmes which consist of a talking head and the equivalent of a blackboard. But comparative costs show a fairly steady pattern. Research carried out within European higher education suggested the ratios set out in Table—5.3. This analysis took as its starting point the fact that teaching material almost always started with a written text so that one could look at the comparative cost of producing material in a variety of formats as compared with the cost of preparing print. These figures are just for production: they do not take account of the reception costs that fall on the learner and leave aside the question of scale already identified.

Table—5.3 Comparative production costs of some technologies

Medium	*Cost per student learning hour in 1998 US $*	*Ratio to print cost*
Print	825	1:1
Radio	24,750 to 44,550	1:50
Television	148,500 to 206,250	1:180 to 250
Audio	280,050	1:35
Video	29,700 to 138,600	1:35 to 1:170
CD-rom	33,000	1:40

Source: Hülsmann 2000

Costs for the new information technologies are only beginning to become available. Here we need to distinguish between the costs for preparing teaching material and for tutoring students on line. American research has indicated a very wide range of costs for preparing material that is presented by computer, with the lowest where this is simply using the computer to present print and the highest where designers move into simulations or virtual reality. The figures, shown in Table—5.4, vary from $6,000 for a simple or $12,000 for a text up to $1,000,000 for a three-unit course. The beginning experience of online tutoring suggests that the costs of this may put strains either on budgets or on tutors' workloads, mainly because there is no ready way of controlling the time tutors spend responding to their students or the demands that students put on their tutors. If there is a computer conference, tutors may feel a responsibility to monitor its contents, regardless of the length of material placed there by students. Where students can contact their tutor by e-mail, they tend to demand more of their tutors' time than when they are submitting a conventional assignment. In the absence of good cost studies of online teaching the only advice for the planner is to welcome the pedagogic advantage of being able to have ready contact with distant students while seeking a way of containing the costs.

Table—5.4 Cost of developing a three-unit internet course 1998

Type of teaching material	*Cost in US$*
Course outlines and assignments	6,000
Text	12,000
Text with reference materials	18,000
Text with reference materials and images	37,500
Audio and video	120,000
Simulations	250,000
Virtual reality	1,000,000

Sources: Arizona Learning Systems 1998

Planner's guidelines for choosing between the options

International experience suggests that the choice of technologies should be guided by five factors:

- Convenience and availability for learners are all important: we need to ensure that the technology does fit with learners' needs and realities.
- Technology needs to be appropriate for the curriculum and for teaching effectiveness. While arguments based on minimising cost, and keeping technology as simple as possible, might often lead us to print, this is not ideal for all purposes and has limitations in terms of motivating students.

- Technical backup and support needs to be in place: it is no good relying on a technology if it cannot be used by students; many videocassettes sitting on shelves in remote villages bear witness to this. Maintenance needs to be planned for.
- The costs need to be affordable for the institution and for the learner.
- There are particular difficulties in achieving a balance here within small states where the use of sophisticated technology may force educators into dependence on external sources with the danger of cultural hegemony by large countries and large international companies.

In general the challenge is to find an appropriate trade-off between quality and cost, justifying any move away from the simplest and cheapest technologies but resisting untested arguments that they are the only ones to be considered.

6

How Can You Fund It?

Much education, at primary, secondary and tertiary levels has conventionally been funded by government and government funding has been the norm for many programmes of initial teacher education and training. But pressure on government funds has led many countries to explore alternative sources of funding so that education is also funded from four other sources: from student fees, community support, the private and non-government sector, and from donors and funding agencies. Programmes often receive funding from a combination of sources: teacher education at a distance in both China and Nigeria, for example, is funded partly by government, partly by student fees. In Brazil, as described in Chapter 3, programme of teacher education has been funded by a combination of private-sector and non-government funding so that the heavy capital costs of television are met by the private sector.

Many governments have been willing to fund not only initial teacher education but some programmes of continuing professional development, especially for curriculum reform or for some upgrading programmes in countries trying to raise the minimum standard of teacher qualification. Teachers are, however, often expected to pay fees where they enrol on a course of continuing professional development which will benefit them in terms of career advancement or salary increment.

Some parts of a programme may be funded by government but not through a ministry of education. If education can get access to state broadcasting time and facilities, at a nominal charge or free of cost, then broadcasting transmission costs do not fall on the ministry of education budget.

What are the consequences of each choice?

There are trade-offs between each of the options. In some jurisdictions there may be an expectation that government should meet the full costs of teacher education because of its importance for the quality of the education service as a whole. Total funding from a ministry of education may hold down available funds and will give the ministry—and its finance section—strong direct control over the programme. There may, therefore, be pressure on the part of the institutions concerned to seek funds outside the ministry or to pass on some of the costs to the learners. On the other hand, the imposition of student fees may hold down enrolment, discourage students, and is likely to be socially regressive. There is little reported experience of the use of community resources in teacher education of this kind. The nature of private-sector and non-government involvement is culturally determined: this sector is involved in the projects in Brazil and at OLSET in South Africa but there are significant differences between the two. The provision in Brazil is through funds generated within the country by an established consortium, while OLSET is dependent on external, donor funding and despite its successes, seems unable to attract government funding. The freedom of action and non-bureaucratic structure that marks effective non-government organisations has bo be balanced against difficulties they may face in integrating their work with regular state activity and ensuring its sustainability.

External finance from funding agencies may also present problems of sustainability. Many funding agencies have been willing to meet capital costs, and to fund pilot projects, but expect governments to meet recurrent and continuing costs. Course development has sometimes, but not always, been treated as capital expenditure even though its major cost element is likely to be for staff time. The trade-off here is often between initial freedom of action, bought with external funds, and long-term integration and sustainability. In seeking that trade-off, it is unwise to brush aside questions about how to maintain a programme or project.

The best advice may be to be open-minded about the options and consider the possibilities of funding different elements of the programme from different sources. Box 6.1 shows how this was done in Malawi.

BOX 6.1 THE MALAWI INTEGRATED IN SERVICE TEACHER EDUCATION PROGRAMME

This project in Malawi brought together funding from a variety of sources including the ministry of education, the World Bank, and the German aid agency GTZ. While some costs undoubtedly fell on the learners, they were not charged fees so that there is no contribution from them shown in this table.

Area of work	*Funding source*
Planning and initiation	MoE (including six professionals from the Teacher Development Unit, experts from Malawi Institute of Education, the University and Colleges of Education). GTZ—long-term expert in logistics.
Materials development	World Bank loan—curriculum review, five handbooks and other learning materials. GTZ—expert in training and materials development, office support costs.
Materials reproduction and distribution	World Bank—printing of training material. GTZ—office support costs and computer equipment.
Reception costs	n/a
Student support and classroom practice	GTZ finances activities for pedagogic support (zonal meeting and school-based supervision) plus vehicles for transport. Colleges (college-based training by tutors, visiting college practical teaching supervisors) conventionally funded by MoE (central MoE for tutor salaries. Regional MoE for accommodating students during college-based phase). MSSSP—transport for PEAs visiting schools.
Training and capacity building	World Bank loan to Malawi (training trainers, PEA's head teachers). Malawi School Support System Programme (MSSSP)—Training Development unit.
Maintenance	GTZ—long-term expert in monitoring and evaluation.

What sort of funds do you need?

Funding is likely to be needed for costs of several different kinds and at different stages in the development of a project of programme. While open and distance learning does not require the building of colleges and halls of residence, it does require some capital investment, for the development of systems and materials, well in advance of student recruitment. This is a critical point which is not necessarily understood in new projects and which can create political and presentational difficulties: once a project has been approved and expectations aroused, it is difficult for planners to insist on a development period of one or two years when, to the outsider or the potential learners, there is little sign of action.

Different activities may be funded from different sources. Costs are likely to be incurred for initial planning, the development of materials, their reproduction and distribution, their reception, student support, training and capacity building, and maintenance.

There are costs associated with initial planning and initiation of teacher education at a distance, even if these amount only to the use of existing capacity within the educational system. These costs have often been funded from regular government budgets. Where programmes are developed with external advice, external funding may be available for planning and initiation. The Asian Development Bank, for example, has funded explorations of the use of open and distance learning for teachers and for initial planning. Agencies like the Commonwealth of Learning have often been involved in the development of plans, sometimes with external funding.

The development of teaching materials, as already noted, requires expenditure before students are enrolled. A variety of strategies has been used for funding this, depending on the organisational structure chosen for the programme (see Chapter 4). Difficulties can arise where teachers or trainers are already in government employment, working in education, but asked to develop materials as an extra or different job. In some cases regulations do not allow them to be paid extra; in others sanctions are impossible if they do not deliver the material. Strategies need to be put in place that allow for the effective development and editing of material that is fair to staff and ensures materials are delivered on time (see Perraton and Creed 1999). Funds for writers are not enough: editing of materials, to ensure their educational effectiveness and get them to camera-ready state or undertake desktop publishing, is likely to cost as much as their initial writing.

The costs for reproducing and distributing teaching materials may fall in various places. If material is broadcast, transmission costs may be met by the broadcasting agency. If learners have to collect materials, some of the costs of distribution fall on them. Where materials are distributed electronically then, once the capital investment has been made, costs to the initiating institution may be negligible.

Costs for reception of materials for an individual learner often fall on the learner, who may be expected to have a radio, or in an industrialised country, to obtain a computer. Where the distance-teaching system brings learners together there may be costs for the development or supply of specialist centres or equipment or negotiations for their use by learners (e.g. the supply of radios, development of videoconference facilities, the use of telecentres).

There will always be costs for the contributing support of students and arrangement for supervision of their classroom practice (where it is likely to be possible to use existing resources within the educational system, providing that the costs, including the opportunity costs, of this are acceptable). In the case of courses undertaken by individuals, in the interest of their own career development, these costs may be covered by a student fee. This element is perhaps the most significant in calculating the recurrent budget and identifying funds for it: it is both a recurrent cost and one that does not allow for economies of scale.

Funds will be needed for training and capacity building, especially as an unfamiliar project is being set up. As with initiation costs, this is an area where funds have often been obtained both from government and from external agencies. These are not, however, once-for-all costs: just as we argued for continuing professional development as an aim of teacher education so it will be necessary for those working in a specialist open and distance learning institution.

Table—6.1 Activities and resources

Activity to be funded	*Type of funding required*	*Comments on possible sources*
Planning and initiation	One-off	May be from MOE funds but often also from funding and international agencies
Materials development	Funding mainly for staff time but can be treated as capital where materials are used over several years.	Upfront funding usually from MOE, ngo or funding agency grants. Funds for revision and updating also required.
Materials reproduction and distribution	Recurrent	Regular expenditure that may be recovered from operating grant or from student fees. Where distribution is through public broadcasting, government mail, or by internet, costs may be borne on other budgets.
Reception costs	May be some capital (e.g. supply of radios, development of videoconference facilities) but recurrent costs then arise	Initial funding may be from one-off grant (e.g. funding agency) Individual recurrent costs (e.g. maintenance of radios, computers) likely to fall on individual learner/centre.
Student support and classroom practice	Recurrent	Regular expenditure that may be recovered from operating grant or from student fees. It may be possible for some costs (e.g. for deployment of school or college staff to support students) to be met from other institutional budgets.
Training and capacity building	Recurrent	Heavy initial expenditure needed, especially where project is unfamiliar to those working in it but continuing expenditure then required.
Maintenance	Recurrent	Continuing expenditure that is often neglected (especially for materials updating) and needs to be built into budgets for previous areas.

Finally, funding is not a once-off activity: maintenance of the whole system, of any equipment, and of teaching materials all incur costs. The costs of maintaining teaching materials, in particular, are often under-estimated at the outset: the effort needed to get them created the first time diverts attention from setting up a programme of continuing revision, improvement and updating.

Table—6.1 shows where resources have most often been located for those activities.

Planners' guidelines for choosing between the options

Distance education for teachers has a patchy record, with many programmes started but abandoned, often because short-term funding arrangements could not be sustained. The record suggests several guidelines.

- The development of open and distance learning for teachers needs to take place within the framework of policy for teacher education generally so that questions about long-term funding are addressed at the outset.
- Even if it is assumed that the bulk of funds will come from government, it is worth considering the options of using alternative sources of funding, examining the trade-offs between them.
- In considering what, if anything, students pay towards a course or programme, it is necessary to balance questions of equity and access (which suggest holding down student fees), questions of motivation (where learners may have medium-term rewards in terms of promotion), and questions of quality (which may demand expenditure above all on student support).
- Remember the maintenance issue.

7

How Do Teachers Learn Practical Skills?

In chapter 1 we distinguished between four functions of teacher education. In one sense, all teacher education needs to be oriented towards the ways in which teacher support children's learning and so to the fourth of those functions, of strengthening teachers' practice in the classroom. But there are differences in the emphasis that has been laid on this function between different programmes. Where these are concerned simply to raise teachers' background education, or where they are designed to help experienced teachers learn about new subject-matter, classroom activities may be downplayed.

In asking about practical skills it is, therefore, legitimate to ask how far this is part of the role of a distance-education programme. The question is critically important for the planner for economic, logistical and educational reasons. The economic ones follow from the fact that the supervision of classroom practice is likely to be labour-intensive and will not show economies of scale. Indeed, if supervisors are to travel and visit teachers in their schools, then the costs of travel may be a significant part of the budget. The logistics are inevitably complicated and likely to involve a partnership of the kind discussed in Chapter 4; a distance-teaching organisation will seldom itself have the staff to undertake this work so that it is likely to involve other partners who in turn need management, support and often training. From the educational point of view, changed activities within the teacher's own classroom are, as we have argued, of the essence of teacher education. This has implications not only for any teaching-practice component within a course but for its structure and content as a whole. Even theoretical elements of a course, including materials presented in print or on radio, can be designed so that they relate to classroom practice. Open and distance learning has a potential advantage in terms of integrating theory and practice where it enables practising teachers to raise their skills by study at a distance and it is worth seeking strategies that will maximise that advantage.

Conventional as well as distance-education progammes have, with varying success, confronted this need to turn what teachers know and believe into what they do to support children's learning. Many conventional programmes fail to attend to this and some produce teachers who are formally qualified but have had only a token or minimal supervised school experience. In some countries, practical teaching forms no part of the final assessment of teachers. The issues for a distance-education provider are about managing the supervision and assessment of students in distant locations and how to design materials and activities in ways which integrate knowledge or theory with practice. In the cases set out in Chapter 3 we have examples of different strategies: a support structure for loca' action-groups of teachers (Brazil), delegation of supervision and assessment to school staff, with varying degrees of prescription and support (Nigeria, Britain, and UNISA in South Africa), the provision of teaching content, models and sequenced structure in the lessons provided for children (OLSET in South Africa), the design of course-work to require a practical application (Britain and Chile), the exchange of practical experience in workshops and newsletters (Mongolia and Brazil) or through websites (Britain and Chile), the demonstration of model lessons through television or video (China), the use of applied projects rather than examinations on theory and the inclusion of the assessment of performance in the final grade on formal programmes (Britain and Nigeria). Some of the projects place the practice of teaching at the centre of programme design and organisation, others assign it a relatively minor, or even marginal, place not because of the logical difficulties involved for a distance education provider but because of the traditions and perceptions of teacher education in the difficult countries, and its role in conventional teacher-education programmes.

In general, strategies to integrate theory with practice fall into the three categories identified by Robinson (1997):

- Knowledge about practice (a teacher is able explain what multi-grade teaching is and produce an essay or examination answer on it);
- Knowledge applied to practice (a teacher can plan the organisation of multi-grade teaching or materials for it and show how these might be used in the situation or report and reflect on work done);
- Demonstration of knowledge and understanding through performance (a teacher shows the use of multi-grade teaching through the conduct of teaching and learning activities, observed by others).

The different categories have different logistical and cost implications for distance education. One danger here is that activities in the first category are (wrongly) assumed by programme providers to result in the outcomes found in the third (competence in performance) as a matter of course. The challenge for the planner is to design a programme so that knowledge is carried through from the first of these to the third and to build in a system of assessment and feedback that tests how successful the programme is in doing so. In many cases this involves more than, say, the integration of work based on classroom activity in assignments or videoconferencing sessions that look at classrooms and requires arrangements for a supervisor to see how teachers are working within their classrooms.

How can it be done?

We can identify five main approaches to the management and supervision of the practicum which are set out in Table—7.1.

For some programmes, an overt or tacit decision has been taken against any formal supervision or assessment of the practicum. This has often been the case, for example, where a programme is mainly concerned to raise learners' background education. In other cases, where programmes are aimed at experienced teachers, there is no formal practical element and therefore no need for a structure to supervise or assess it. The Certificate in Guidance by IGNOU,

Table—7.1 Models of organising the practicum in teacher training by distance programmes

Model	*Examples*
1. No practicum offered at all	Certificate in Guidance, IGONU (India)
2. College-based micro-teaching	Belize Teacher Training College
3. Classroom-based practicum as a separate block ina course, usually placed after academic blocks.	Diploma in Education, IGNOU (India),
4. Classroom-based practicum supervised by visiting staff from college or ministry	Zimbabwe ZINTEC project
5. Classroom-based practicum under the guidance of a mentor within the school	Open University (Britain) Postgraduate Certificate of Education

for example, inserts into the theoretical work suggestions about how to extend the ideas presented in the units into classroom practice but this is purely voluntary and not formally assessed.

In the second model, within programmes such as that of the Belize teachers' college referred to above the only practical work consists of college-based microteaching. This cuts down sustainability on the organisational headaches of a school-based practicum but severely limits supervision and guidance of trainees' actual teaching.

The third model offers the practicum as a separate block of classroom-based teaching. The Indira Gandhi National Open University offers a Diploma in Education, for example, which has a one-off block of practical teaching after all the theoretical units. The government of Ghana has explored a model of teacher education in which students spend blocks of time working in a conventional college and blocks studying at a distance while they are working in school. This approach has the benefit of logistical simplicity, and allows cohorts of students to move from one mode of study to another. It does, however, run the risk that theory, done in one block of time, is unrelated to practice, done in another and that the guidance offered by tutors in colleges is seen as irrelevant by student teachers once they are working in schools. Close integration between the theoretical units and their practical pedagogical application becomes more difficult.

In the fourth model, trainee teachers follow a course while they are teaching and are visited, from time to time, by a supervisor from the college or from some other part of the teaching service. School inspectors, for example, have often been given this role. In principle this should make it possible both to integrate learning at a distance with practical classroom applications. In practice, logistical difficulties have often been overwhelming: in Zimbabwe, where this model was used, evaluation showed that supervision of this kind was the weakest part of the programme so that nearly all the students participating in one evaluation thought that field supervision was inadequate. Where inspectors were deployed to supervise, they had to change their, role sometimes with difficulty. Even college lecturers were reported to 'spend more time checking schemes of work and lessons plans rather than assisting students in the reinforcement of concepts, skills and linking theory with practice' (Chivore 1993: 59).

In the fifth model, school based teaching is an integral part of the course, interspersed and often closely integrated with the theoretical units, and is supervised by a school-based monitor. In the case of the British Open University, outlined in Chapter 3, the university decided to decentralise the supervision of classroom practice to individual schools. This was seen as a necessary strategy to enable students to enrol on the course regardless of where they were living but it also fitted with current national policy of moving towards school-based teacher education. The university undertook the job of briefing and training mentors, who were regular members of the staff of schools throughout the country, and paid them a fee which was a substantial proportion of the total expenditure on the course. The work of mentors themselves was supervised by the staff of the university's education faculty, working from its regional offices.

Where can it be done?

These five models locate teaching practice in different places. Management difficulties are minimised where it is centralised, as in the Belize example, which also made it possible to use relatively advanced—and expensive—television techniques for microteaching. If teachers are supervised in their own schools, by someone from the distance-teaching institution or one of its partners, it should in principle be easier to ensure an integration between theory and practice. While in many instances there have been logistical difficulties in supervising classroom practice in this way either the third or fourth model is one that has most often been seen as appropriate and realistic.

The fifth model, of employing school-based, mentors has attracted widespread interest. It depends on the availability of teachers within the system who have themselves sufficient experience and understanding of education to act as mentors, and a structure to brief and train them and to monitor their work. Many ministries of education, in considering this option, have rejected it as unrealistic as these conditions cannot be met. It has also been criticised as a system which served to replicate the existing culture and values of the schools where the mentors and their trainee teachers are working. On the other hand, in discussing their experience, the Open University argued that their school-based approach meant that it was possible to ensure:

> that all the open and distance test and resources should be directly related to school practice. No activity, regarding or observation could be set that did not directly relate to experience in schools: the link had to be explicit. The course, therefore, also prescribes a *curriculum of school activities*... This school activities framework is directly related to the course structure and assessment model and allows for increasingly demanding activities, covering all aspects of the teaching role, as the programme progresses.
>
> *Moon* and *Leach* 1997: 5

Planners' guidelines for choosing between the options

This chapter has argued consistently the importance of asking how teachers will apply what they themselves learn in their classroom, leading to the following proposals.

- Examine critically how far teachers will demonstrate and understand through their own performance the material they have been working on in their course.
- Plan appropriate arrangements for supervision of classroom practice in the light of that examination. Take account of the logistics and budget needed for this element.

- Explore where there are people or institutions who can help in managing and supervising classroom practice which will often necessitate a partnership with other institutions.
- Consider the balance of advantages of the options for the practice of teaching skills, their location, and the issues of who should supervise them and how those people should be supervised and trained.

8

How Can We Assess It?

There are three separate issues here: how we can make an assessment of open and distance learning as a whole; how we can build in a system of assessment or formative evaluation of quality control within the institution; how we can assess education for teachers. In the context of teacher education we look in particular detail at the last of these.

How do we assess open and distance learning?

In trying to assess the distance-education experience we are limited by the shortage of good evaluation. One can speculate as to why. Sometimes critical evaluations exist but are difficult to access because they are internal and confidential reports. Sometimes excellent evaluations that are in the public domain are buried within rabbit-warren generalist websites. But the overriding impression here is that distance and teacher education, both together and separately, and under-researched and under-theorised areas and particularly so in developing countries (Robinson, 1997). The dearth of evaluative literature seems partly to do with the difficulties of assessing a complex and interrelated range of factors related to effectiveness. The way that distance education disperses responsibility for a programme among a range of partners, sometimes on a large—scale over distance for student support, administration, tutoring, course production, delivery and assessment—presents a number of logistical and methodological challenges for researchers. In many countries it is hampered by limited research capacity and expertise, limited research culture, and limited funding. In programmes with a wide geographical reach, data from the centre often cannot tell us how well it is working at more local levels. Often the means for gathering data is problematic: researchers on the project in Chile (see Chapter 3) commented that: "The main constraint for researching the programme is the lack of an organised database with information about it. Even though the staff was open and willing to help, they did not have an easy way of getting some information and in some cases their memory was the only source available" (Cerda, Leon and Ripoll forthcoming).

In many countries it is hampered by limited research capacity and expertise, limited research culture, and limited funding. Funding may be the key: education spends less on research and evaluation than many other areas of human enterprise. The result is that policy-makers have very little critical information on which to make informed decisions about teacher education by distance and providers have limited feedback from within their institutions to improve their practice.

Many evaluations have been narrowly focused, too. Studies of a necessary breadth "demand intensive work on the ground and a greater commitment to evaluation than many authorities have felt able to give. For the most part, therefore, we have to rely on much more partial evidence" (Robinson 1997: 133). We know that distance-education methods can be used on a scale that makes a difference to national numbers in teacher supply but we do not know enough in terms of its effectiveness, curriculum and cost.

We have suggested, in Chapter 2, the need to look at student numbers and completion rates, about evidence on learning gain or examination success, and about the effect of programmes on classroom practice and then, in order to make comparisons with conventional approaches, about costs. In all these areas we are short of data and evidence-based decisions about appropriate methodologies suffer as a result. More research and better research will make for better practice.

How do we provide for quality control and formative evaluation?

Formative evaluation is likely to strengthen any educational institution. It has a particular significance for open and distance learning partly because its methods are complex and likely to involve many partners and partly because its students are distant, unseen, and often unheard. It is, therefore, necessary to build measures for quality assessment into all the processes of a distance-teaching institution. Many general guides on open and distance learning give advice on this which is not significantly different for teacher education from education for their purposes. In introducing a set of guidelines developed for higher education in Britain, for example, the Quality Assurance Agency has argued:

> System design, programme and delivery, student development and support, student communication and representation, and student assessment all raise particular questions for institutions about the ways in which they 'manage' teaching and learning to ensure that the quality of provision and security of academic standards are as they need to be...
>
> Distance learning must rely on a sound and effective logistical and administrative infrastructure to ensure that all participants' activities are co-ordinated and engage with the programme as designed by the provider. There is likely to be a distinct division of labour both in teaching and administration. An integral part of the teaching and administrative system is the timing of action and the lead times needed to meet deadlines. The guidelines place particular emphasis on these points.
>
> *Higher Education Quality Council* 1999

It goes on to propose that quality assurance should be examined under six headings: system design; programme design, approval and review; management of programme delivery; student development and support; student communication and representation; and student assessment. We examine that last of these below as it presents particular difficulties in teacher education. Of the other areas, distance-teaching institutions have been particularly concerned to create appropriate systems to monitor system design, the development of teaching materials, and student support.

In assessing alternative proposals for system design it is necessary to examine how open and distance learning articulates with the rest of the educational system so that it provides a quality of education that matches the needs of students which is recognised as being on a par with conventional education. Furthermore, it demands a structure that monitors the processes of distance education to ensure that they are working effectively and efficiently for learners. Academic quality of the work at the centre is not enough: institutions also need to know how well their systems are working for communicating with students, for sending and responding to their work, and for maintaining student records.

There is now an extensive literature on the development of effective teaching materials for open and distance learning, in a range of different media, and a measure of agreement on the principles that underline good instructional design. In designing an assessment system it is therefore appropriate to build in checks on the development and presentation of materials to ensure that they are pedagogically effective.

We have touched on some of the issues involved in ensuring effective student support in Chapter 7 on classroom practice. Where teachers, studying at a distance, have themselves little experience as adult learners, or of learning outside a conventional classroom, they are likely to need considerable support, offered through written comments on assignments, or electronically, or through face-to-face contact with tutors. Measures to monitor the quality and timeliness of this work need to be built into the system.

How do we assess distance education for teachers?

In Chapter 7, in relation to teaching practice, we distinguished between three levels of teachers' knowledge and practice. In a valuable review of the problems, Robinson has proposed the nature of assessment appropriate to each and its implications for distance education (Robinson 1997: 130-3). She points out that the difficulties of assessing students working through distance education parallel the difficulties in using it for teaching. Distinguishing three levels of assessment, as in Table—8.1, she points out:

> Knowledge and understanding are easier for a distance education provider to assess than practice and performance. Assessment of a student's pedagogical skills, the outcomes, is difficult for distance educators to do alone since it needs first-hand observation and authentication. As the model in Table [8.1] shows it becomes more complex organisationally for a distance education provider and the costs rise, as assessment moves from Level 1 (knowledge and understanding) to Level 3 (practice and performance), that is from standard patterns of assessment of knowledge for large groups to assessment of individual performance and difference. One strength of distance education is its capacity to deal with large numbers, one limitation is its inability to deal easily with the individual.
>
> *Robinson 1997*

Table—8.1 Assessing teachers' knowledge and practice at a distance

Teachers' knowledge and practice	*Nature of assessment*	*Implications for distance education*
Level 1: Knowledge and understanding Of academic subjects to be taught Of pedagogical concepts, ideas and theory	Written work (assignments), essays, course tests, final examinations.	Can assess learning and give feedback to students on a large scale (hundreds or thousands). Can achieve economies of scale (standard assignments.) Can provide well-designed assignments because of the resource put into course design; may also retreat into over-use of multiple-choice questions for administrative convenience. Assignments may remain too theoretical or unrelated to the realities of classroom life, or lack regional relevance.
Level 2: Knowledge applied to practice Application of knowledge to teachers' own context; testing out and interpreting ideas about pedagogy; evaluating practical activities and experiments, and reflecting on them	Written reports and accounts of things done (description and analysis of activities such as teaching a mathematical topic a new way; collecting evidence in a child observation study; organising a classroom differently; or developing new language and reading activities).	Good learning materials can structure this process for the teacher (distance not a barrier). Can support linkage between theory and practice. Not possible for a distance education provider to tell from the student's reports how authentic an account is given, for example, that classroom practice matches what is described. Can be more time-consuming and expensive for a distance education provider to assess (non-standard assignments, greater individual differences).

(Contd...)

Teachers' knowledge and practice	*Nature of assessment*	*Implications for distance education*
Level 3: Practice and performance Enactment of knowledge and ideas Demonstration of competences and skills	Direct observation and authentication of individual teacher performance	Much more complex to organise and manage than Level 1. More labour-intensive and expensive than Level 1; approximates more closely to costs of conventional training. Requires more support staff in a variety of roles than Level 1; needs more staff training provision; more support materials; more monitoring and management. Needs local partners. Cannot be done at a distance (without sophisticated interactive technologies).

Source: Robinson 1997

If we want to assess teachers' knowledge and understanding, which may be the main aim of a programme that concentrates on improving teachers' general education or their knowledge in one particular area, then there are no particular difficulties in assessing them through conventional tests and at a distance. Assessment can be built into written work relatively easily. Several of the projects discussed in section 3 arranged for assessment of this kind. It becomes more difficult if we move up one level and ask how far teachers are applying their knowledge to practice. It is, however, still possible to design learning materials, in a variety of media, that ask teachers to undertake activities in the classroom and report on them. This kind of student assignment makes it possible for the tutor both to guide the student and to assess how far knowledge has in fact been applied to practice. The third level, in which we ask how far teachers are in fact applying what they have learned in the classroom, is both the most difficult to manage and, as argued in the previous chapter, often the most important. Just as managing and supervising classroom practice presents particular difficulties for open and distance learning so does its assessment. Again, if this centrally important kind of assessment is to be undertaken, a distance-teaching institution needs to work with partners on the ground, who will themselves need guidance and possibly training in their work. Efforts have been made, using a variety of approaches, to arrange this. The National Teachers' Institute in Nigeria produced a standard grid for assessment of classroom practice by external supervisors. At the British Open University, assessment of teaching practice, throughout the course, was a responsibility of the mentor and school co-ordinator. Students were required to keep a 'professional development portfolio' which included school practice assessments made by the mentor, which was submitted to the university at the end of the course for marking.

Like reconnaissance, time spent on the assessment of individual teacher assessment is never wasted.

Guidelines for planners

Assessment tends to be neglected. This chapter argues:

- Formative evaluation needs to provide information about the quality open and distance learning generally, about the quality of the processes of a distance-teaching institution, and about the assessment of individual teachers.
- More good research is to be encouraged in order to guide practice.
- Systems of quality, control need to address themselves to: system design, programme design and delivery, student development and support, student communication and representation, and student assessment.
- There are particular needs to look at the monitoring of day-to-day practice within the institutional system, at teaching materials, and at student support as well as at the assessment of individual teachers.
- This needs to look at the problems, in increasing organisational complexity, of assessing knowledge and understanding, knowledge applied to practice, and practice and performance.

References

Arizona Learning Systems, 1998, *Preliminary Cost Methodology for Distance Learning*, Arizona Learning Systems and the State Board of Directors for Community College of Arizona.

Avalos, B., 1991, *Approaches to Teacher Education: Initial Teacher Training*, London: Commonwealth Secretariat.

Beeby, C.E., 1996, *The Quality of Education in Developing Countries*, Cambridge Mass: Harvard University Press.

Cerda, C., Leon, M. and Ripoll, M., forthcoming, 'Teachers Learning to use Information Technology in Chile' in UNESCO *International Case Studies of Teacher Education through Distance Learning* (provisional title), Paris.

Chale, E. M., 1993, 'Tanzania's Distance-Teaching Programme', in Perraton, 1993.

Chivore, B.R.S.,1993, 'The Zimbabwe Integrated Teacher Education Course', in Perraton, 1993.

Clark, R.E., 1993, 'Reconsidering Research on Learning from Media', *Review of Education Research* 53, 4: 445-59.

Department for International Development, 2001, Imfundo: Partnership for IT in Education Inception Report, London.

Greenland, J, 1993, (ed.), The In-Service Training of Primary School Teachers in English-Speaking Africa: A report, Basingstoke: Macmillan.

Hülsmann, T., 2000, The Costs of Open Learning: A Handbook, Oldenburg: BIS, University of Oldenburg.

Mählck, L. and Temu, E. B., 1989, *Distance Versus College Trained Primary School Teachers: A Case Study from Tanzania Paris*: International Institute for Educational Planning.

Moon, B. and Leach, J., 1997, 'Towards a New Generation of Open Learning Programmes in Teacher Education: the Open University (UK) Pre-Service Teacher Education Programme', Paper Presented to the *Distance Education for Teacher Development Colloquium, Global Knowledge 1997 Conference*, Toronto, 22-25 June.

Nielsen, H.D. and Tatto, M.T., 1993, 'Teacher Upgrading in Sri Lanka and Indonesia' in Perraton, 1993.

Perraton, H., 1993, (ed.) *Distance Education for Teacher Training, London*: Toutledge.

Perraton, H., 2000, *Open and Distance Learning in the Developing World*, London: Routledge.

Perraton, H. 2001 'Quality and Standards of INSET Teacher Training by Open and Distance Learning', paper presented to the Pan-African Dialogue on In-Service Teacher Training by Open and Distance Learning, Windhoek, Namibia-9-12, July 2001.

Perraton, H. and Creed, C. ,1999, *Distance Education Practice: Training and Rewarding Authors*, London: DFID Education Research Series, No. 33.

Perraton, H. and Creed, C., 2000, *Applying New Technologies and Cost-Effective Delivery Systems in Basic Education* (Thematic Study for Education for All 2000 Assessment). Paris: UNESCO.

Quality Assurance Agency for Higher Education, 1999, Distance Learning Guidelines, Gloucester (http://www.qaa.ac.uk/public/dlg/contents.htm, accessed 3 December 2001).

Robinson, B., 1997, 'Distance Education for Primary Teacher Training in Developing Countries', in ed. Lynch, J. et al. *Innovations in Delivering Primary Education Vol. III of Education and Development: Tradition and Innovation*, London: Cassell.

Robinson, B., Creed, C. and Parraton, H., 2001, *Teacher Education through Distance Learning: Technology, Curriculum, Cost, Evaluation*, Paris: UNESCO.

Russell, T. and McPherson, S., 2001, 'Indicators of Success in Teacher Education: A Review and Analysis of Recent Research', Paper Presented to Pan-Canadian Education Research Agenda Symposium on Teacher Education/Educator Training, Québec: Université Laval, 22-23 May.

Torres, R.M., 1996, 'Without the Reform of Teacher Education There will be no Reform of Education', *Prospects* 26, 3: 447-67.

Appendix

TEACHER EDUCATION THROUGH DISTANCE LEARNING: CASE STUDIES

Introduction

The world needs better teachers and more teachers. The Dakar conference revealed that there were still more than 100 million children out of school: they need teachers as the world moves towards the 2015 target of education for all. And we need to raise the skills of the existing 60 million teachers, too many of whom are untrained and unqualified. Beyond that, the skills and knowledge all teachers need are no longer fixed and familiar targets but moving ones. Teachers therefore need more opportunities than ever before to go on learning throughout their careers. One of the ways of strengthening the teaching profession is to use distance education or open and distance learning.

Why the case studies

UNESCO commissioned this set of case studies because of demands from member states for guidance on implementing programmes of distance education for teachers. The studies are therefore, intended to document experience on which to base the *Guidelines for Teacher Education at a Distance*, a separate document from this, to be published in 2002.

More specifically we wanted to find out what open and distance learning was being used for in teacher education, how effectively it was working, and what methods it was using. In asking how effectively it was working, we wanted to examine its record in attacking the major problems confronting teacher education. There are two kinds of questions here: about effectiveness and about relevance. To gauge effectiveness we were looking for data on completion rates and comparative costs and for any indicators of effects on the work of teachers in the classroom or the community. To assess relevance we wanted to discover whether the initiatives were a significant sustainable, part of the service of teacher education or a small, peripheral, activity with little chance of making any major impact on the problems.

If open and distance learning for teachers is effective, and working on a big enough scale to be actually or potentially significant, then it is worth going on to ask how it is managed. We, therefore, went on to ask about the curriculum of open and distance learning initiatives, and the extent to which this matches that of other forms of teacher education and professional development. We also looked at organisational structures, and the kinds of organisations that provide teacher-education programmes, and the different patterns of funding. We looked at the technologies, ranging from print to computers, and the relationship between work done through the technologies and work done face-to-face, including all-important issues about classroom practice.

Educational needs and problems

Many countries still do not have enough teachers. In some, the expansion needed in the teaching force is far beyond the capacity of traditional colleges. The supply of teachers is also adversely affected in countries where retention rates one low for newly trained teachers or where significant numbers of teachers are being lost through HIV-AIDS or in rural areas which have difficulties in recruiting and retaining teachers.

Teacher quality is an issue in most countries. Many teachers are untrained or underqualified or teaching subjects in which they are not qualified or trained. In addition, teachers face a widening range of demands and roles. National governments, international organisations and specific circumstances continually set new goals: gender parity by 2005 and universal basic education by 2015; inclusive education; education for democracy, peace and social cohesion; multi-grade teaching; increased accountability for achieving learning targets; the development of learners who are self-managing and independent, skilled in critical thinking and problem solving, equipped with life-skills; the preparation of learners who are competent for knowledge-based economies, capable in the use of information technology; and the expansion of teachers' roles to include social work in communities where child-headed households and orphans one common as a result of HIV-AIDS.

The attention given to teacher education and their continuing professional development has in many cases lagged behind that given to other parts of the education system. Some countries lack a policy for it, though the importance of teachers is emphasised in many international reports (e.g., UNESCO 1998, UNESCO 2000, OECD 2001). Although there is wide recognition that teacher education, training and professional development need to be integrated, in ways that operationalise lifelong learning for teachers, the resources allocated to it are usually inadequate and the opportunities too few. In some countries teachers can expect one week's in-service professional development once every five to ten years. On average, countries spend around one per cent of their annual education expenditure on the continuing professional development of teachers (business and industry typically spend 6 per cent on staff development).

All of this creates new challenges for teacher education and continuing professional development: the need to find ways of using existing resources differently, of expanding access to learning opportunities at affordable cost, of providing alternative pathways to initial teacher training of drawing on new constituencies of the population to work as teachers, of using technologies appropriately to enrich a teachers' context and support practice, of stimulating and supporting teachers' active learning and of reconceptualising the traditional organisation of initial teacher education and continuing development.

Can open and distance learning respond to these challenges? The case studies here offer some answers, in describing a range of uses of open and distance learning for both initial and continuing teacher education, using a variety of technologies.

The case studies

Initial teacher education and training is the programme of studies which leads to qualified teacher status according to the official standards of a country. It is the basic or first level of qualification for a teacher. It may be taken as a pre-service programme (before a trainee teacher begins work as a teacher) or an in-service one (while an untrained teacher is working as a teacher).

Continuing professional development enables teachers to expand existing knowledge and skills and develop new ones. Some of this takes the form of long structured courses leading to formal qualifications (diplomas or bachelor's degrees). Other forms are shorter, concentrate on skills in managing children's learning or curriculum change and do not lead to additional qualifications. In some countries, qualified and unqualified teachers alike participate in continuing professional development. It may be provided as in-service activities (on-the-job learning) or out-of-school courses of varying lengths (off-the-job or in vacations).

We have categorised the case studies in four ways.

First, some countries have used distance education to provide a route to initial qualifications for significant numbers of teachers, both new entrants to teaching and experienced unqualified teachers. The China Television Teachers' College and the National Teachers' Institute in Nigeria have long experience of this approach and have become a recognised and institutionalised part of the regular education system in their countries. In a programme that reflects an official policy shift towards more school-based training, the Open University in Britain has run a school-based qualifying programme for graduates who want to enter teaching but have had no professional teacher training.

Second, initial teacher education is no longer seen as enough. Distance education is, therefore, also being used to raise the skills, deepen the understanding and extend the knowledge of teachers. Some programmes are broadly focused while others are targeted at specialist groups. Programmes are taken either by individuals or by groups of teachers who are encouraged to participate by their schools or their employers, as can be seen in these case studies. For example, a non-profit television station is taking the lead on supporting school groups in Brazil. In other cases, programmes are available for individual teachers who want to improve their skills and their status, often enrolling on an individual basis, and at their own expense. Indira Gandhi National Open University in India has a number of programmes of this kind of which its

Certificate in Guidance is one. The University of South Africa also offers programmes on this basis.

Their B.Ed. programmes are for experienced underqualified teachers and also new entrants to teaching, which serve to meet individual goals as well as contributing to the policy goal of a graduate teaching force. Some programmes are aimed at the upgrading of teachers' qualifications required by official policy as new standards are set in a country (as in China).

Third, distance education can have a role in programmes of curriculum reforms which aim to change either the content or the process of education. In South Africa, the Open Learning Systems Educational Trust is using radio to improve the teaching of English, and to support teachers in this work. In Mongolia, radio and print are used across large distances to reorient teachers to official changes in curriculum and teaching methods within a country in transition. In response to policy initiatives aimed at establishing the use of ICT in schools, the Universidad de la Frontera in Chile is using ICT to support teachers who are teaching these subjects.

Fourth, distance education has been used for teachers' career development. As they seek promotion, or aim for the next qualification level, or aspire to become a head teacher, or work in a teachers' college, or become an inspector, teachers need to acquire new skills. At multinational distance education project in West Africa has developed a training programme in school management for head teachers and aspiring heads.

These categories inevitably overlap: career development may be regarded as part of continuing professional development; it blurs a distinction between the initial education of new recruits to teaching and of experienced but unqualified teachers. Some of the programme have more than one audience, qualified and unqualified teachers, teachers studying for initial qualifications and those using the same programme to upgrade their qualifications.

In general, distance education programmes have been developed with varied intentions: of widening access to teaching qualifications; of disseminating good practice; of strengthening the education system as a whole by reaching not only teachers but the wider community; in enabling school-based training and professional development and as a means of strengthening the links between theory and practice, focusing on the school as a site of teachers' learning. The case studies (listed in Table—1) reflect these purposes.

Background: open and distance learning

Distance education has been used to teach, support and develop teachers for many years: UNESCO was a pioneer through its UNRWA/UNESCO Institute of Education which was training teachers for refugees forty years ago. While the success of programmes has varied, experience demonstrates that distance education can be used to enable teachers to learn and to gain qualifications. The use of new information and communication technologies has drawn new attention to open and distance learning and offers new possibilities.

Distance education has been defined as an educational process in which a significant proportion of the teaching is conducted by someone removed in space and/or time from the learner. Open learning, in turn, is an organised educational activity, based on the use of teaching materials, in which constraints on study are minimised in terms either of access, or of time and place, pace, method of study, or any combination of these. The term 'open and distance learning' is used as an umbrella term to cover educational approaches of this kind that reach teachers in their schools, provide learning resources for them, or enable them to qualify without attending college in person, or open up new opportunities for keeping up-to-date no matter where or when they want to study. The flexibility inherent in open and distance learning, and the fact that it can be combined with a full or near full-time job, makes it particularly appropriate for the often widely-distributed force of teachers and school managers. Some open and distance learning programmes lead to a qualification, others do not; some are addressed to individuals and others to groups; some are tightly organised and others essentially a way of making learning resources available to teachers. All fall under this one umbrella of open and distance learning.

Table—1 The case studies

Category	*Cases*	*Technologies*
Initial qualifications Programmes leading to qualified teacher status.	An alternative route to primary teacher qualifications. Nigeria	Print with face-to-face meetings.
	Using ICT to support school-based initial teacher education, United Kingdom	Print, computer communications, face-to-face meetings, video and audio, written feedback on assignments.
	Reaching teachers through television, China	Television and video copies some print, audio-cassettes, face-to-face classes or meetings.
Continuing professional development Programmes and activities extending teachers' knowledge, skills and expertise throughout a teacher's working life	Television-plus, journalism in the service of teacher development, Brazil	Television and video copies, magazines, newsletters, telephone 'call-in' centre, face-to face meetings.
	New routes to teacher education degrees. South Africa	Print with some face-to-face meetings, audio-and video-cassettes and some small optional element of computer communications.
	Developing primary teachers' knowledge and skills in child guidance, India	Print, face-to-face meetings and some audio-and video-cassettes.

(*Contd...*)

Category	*Cases*	*Technologies*
Re-orientation of teachers for curriculum reform and change Supporting teachers in changing what they teach and how they teach it.	Interactive radio for supporting teachers of English as a second language, South Africa	Radio programmes, audio-cassette copies, print and some face-to-face meetings.
	Reorienting primary teachers to new teaching approaches. Mongolia	Print and audio (radio and audio-cassettes), some videos and face-to-face meetings.
	Teachers learning to use information technology. Chile	Computer communications for an online programme, for delivering materials, supporting interaction, providing access to databases and submitting coursework.
Teacher's career development Programmes to extend the careers of qualified teachers.	Professional development of head teachers in Burkina Faso	Print and face-to-face meetings.

Note: The technologies listed in Table—1 are those used for delivering the programme. More are used in developing the materials or, in some cases, in training tutors, and computers play a large role in materials development and production.

The following are the summaries of the ten case studies taken up to study different aspects of 'teacher education through distance learning'.

Television-Plus: Journalism in the Service of Teacher Development, Brazil

A-Plus is a daily television series designed to stimulate interest in education, teaching and learning among teachers and in the broader community. Taking a journalistic approach, it uses a private educational television channel to reach an audience of 13 million across Brazil. It also helps mobilise teachers into follow-up action through its Community Mobilisation Networks.

The context

The Brazilian educational system has large number of primary and secondary teachers who have low levels of education. The poor quality of many teachers has been a matter of concern. As a result, many initiatives have been taken by a variety of state and private providers for in-service teacher development. Teachers in Brazil are well-provided with all kinds of professional development opportunities though their relevance and effectiveness one sometimes questioned. Many of the initiatives offer distance education, usually print and other media. Some of the providers are non-governmental organisations (NGOs) and private sector organisations. One of these is TV-Futura, a non-profit educational television channel sponsored by a consortium of 14 public and private institutions. TV-Futura ('The Learning Channel') has sponsored the popular A-Plus television series. The target audience is educators at large: primary teachers but also parents, social workers, nurses, childcare providers, and the community. TV-Futura states that its mission starts when the broadcast ends so one of its goals is to mobilise viewers (especially teachers) through its Community Mobilisation Network.

The programme

Its purpose is to help educators deal more critically and effectively with practical matters of concern to them and the community. The 15-minute daily TV programmes have a magazine format, combining general educational news with an in-depth documentary. Each programmes shows two examples of real-life applications of the programme topic, for example, a method of literacy teaching or using videos in the classroom or conducting PTA meetings. An education expert comments in a challenging way on the examples or presents arguments designed to lead viewers to reflect. Suggestions for further activities and references to other sources of information are given at the end of each broadcast. Twice a week, the programme is supplemented by two sets of commentaries, one based on relevant research, the other introducing literature to help viewers apply the topic in real-life situations. Follow-on activities and monthly meetings are organised around these programmes for teachers' groups that opt in to the 'plus' part of the programme. A-Plus provides 60 Community Officers who facilitate the Community Mobilisation Network which supports this activity. The programme has no set curriculum but aims to be responsive to teachers' needs, drawing on several sources of guidance.

Brazil		
Population (millions)		168.2
Size ('000km²)		8,547
GDP per capita (purchasing power parity US $)		7,037
Human Development Index		0.750
Educational data	*Primary*	*Secondary*
Teaching force total '000	1,388,247	326,827
'000 female	–	
Gross enrolment ratio		
All students	125	56
Female	–	–
Pupil-teacher ratio	24	–

Source: UNDP 2001; UNESCO 2000; UNESCO 2001

Note: Population size, GDP and HDI figures are for 1999; Education figures are 1996

Media and technology

A-Plus programmes are broadcast daily by TV-Futura, the philanthropic division of the GLOBO communications network in Brazil. Television was chosen to provide national coverage, build on a tradition of educational television in Brazil and exploit the high ownership of televisions at home and in schools (36 million out of 40 million households and 50 per cent of 118,000 urban schools have it). Production standards are high and its status as an independent provider helps it take a broad approach to programme content, avoiding adherence to a particular pedagogic doctrine. Some urban schools video-record the programmes though rural schools are less equipped to do this. From 2001, local TV stations will be able to rebroadcast the programmes. There are two main categories of audience; a general pay-TV audience (a potential 40 million) and the captive audience of institutions and educators that have joined the Community Mobilisation Network. Print is used for a bi-monthly Network newsletter and a quarterly magazine for viewers, giving schedules and background reading.

Funding and costs

TV-Futura has an annual budget of US $78.7 million, financed by 14 sponsors, including private national and multinational firms and chambers of industry. Its financing structure determines the budget of specific programmes. Budgets cover costs for staff and development but not facilities for production, broadcasting, administrative and infrastructure costs. Like other TV programmes, A-Plus has high front-end production costs and low per user costs. The average cost of a 15-minute programme includes US $1,750.00 direct production costs, US $750.00 indirect costs and US $1,000.00 travel costs (on location). Broadcast costs are 2 per cent of total costs or a few cents per viewer per year. The annual cost of the Community Mobilisation Network is US $720,000 for the total officers (av. US $12,000.00 per officer). On present participation figures this amounts to annual unit costs of US $84 per institution, US $18 per teacher and 60 cents per potential beneficiary. Cost per viewer (based on 7 million per day and a daily transmission cost of US $24,000.00) is less than 10 cents per viewer per programme. Participating institutions receive free cabling by TV-Futura or receivers by NET SKY (6.3 million subscriptions in January 2001). TV-Futura is a high-risk and vulnerable initiative since it relies totally on private funding and being an educational channel, it cannot sell advertising. However, there is potential for fund-raising through joint ventures.

Quality, effectiveness and outcomes

The programmes have a large regular viewing audience. Surveys reveal 13 million regular viewers, mainly teachers (60 per cent) but also parents, social workers, nurses and child carers. Most (78 per cent) view at home and 12 per cent in schools. Reasons given for viewing include personal development (65 per cent), to get lesson plans (39 per cent), to stimulate classroom discussion (30 per cent), as background material for homework (26 per cent) and for content information (14 per cent). About 70 per cent of viewers are women.

The Community Mobilization Network is active. It currently includes 8,600 participating institutions (schools, hospitals and prisons). Schools are 90 per cent of participating institutions and serve a potential 1,200,000 educators. So far, 40,000 teachers and educators have participated in training and other Network activities. The programmes are exploited in different ways in different regions but appropriate to their schools and communities. Through these activities, teachers have also become familiar with the use of video for educational purposes.

Although there is no hard data about how much is learned and used by teachers, there is plenty of evidence that the programme communicates with them, addresses relevant needs, prompts varied action and suggests new approaches. Unlike many of the other professional development programmes, A-Plus allows teachers to observe, discuss, probe and interact with what other teachers are doing or trying to do. It addresses educational issues determined by teacher interest rather than educational authorities. Its pedagogy encourages educators to reflect on a variety of educational approaches and to extend their practices in ways that include community involvement. Its content avoids domination by a particular educational dogma but draws on many points of view and sources.

Professional Development of Head-Teachers in Burkina Faso

In association with RESAFAD (the African Network for Education at a Distance) Burkina Faso has developed a course for the in-service professional development of head-teachers. The programme benefited from the use of new information and communication technologies to help the process of course development but used print, coupled with meetings of head-teachers, to reach its scattered audience. Over four years it reached about a quarter of Burkina Faso's head teachers.

The context

More than 80 per cent of Burkina Faso's population is rural so that its schools are widely scattered, some of them being many kilometres from district education offices. The need to develop in-service programmes for head teachers was recognised at a meeting of ministers of education in 1992 and carried forward by RESAFAD in a joint programme initially involving Burkina Faso, Guinea, Mali and Togo. Distance education was identified as an appropriate methodology to reach head teachers, and to offer them professional upgrading without their having to lose their jobs.

The programme

The intention of the programme was to strengthen the management capacity of head-teachers. The programme contained material on pedagogy, practical teaching, educational principles and values, environment and the local community, concentrating above all on school management. Plans for the course were developed in association with RESAFAD, which works to develop regional uses of distance education, and with the other member countries in the region. But the materials used with Burkina Faso were developed in-country by the staff of teachers' colleges there, who received training about distance education through RESAFAD. Three cohorts of head-teachers went through the programme between 1997 and 2000. The programme concentrated on the heads of larger schools—those with more than three classes. The head teachers themselves had varied background education: while a small number had a university diploma some had no more than six years of primary and three years of junior secondary education. The programme did not lead to any formal qualification but this is not reported to have caused difficulty or raised objections.

Burkina Faso		
Population (millions)		11.2
Size ('000 km²)		274
GDP per capita (purchasing power parity US$)		965
Human Development Index		0.320
Educational data	*Primary*	*Secondary*
Teaching force	14,037[a]	
total '000		..
'000 female	3,412[a]	–
Gross enrolment ratio		
All students	40	–
Female	31	–
Pupil-teacher ratio	50	–

Source: UNDP 2001; UNESCO 2000; UNESCO 2001

Note: Population size, GDP, and HDI figures are for 1999, Education figures are 19996

Media and technology

In view of the limited communications infrastructure of Burkina Faso it was decided to use the simplest technologies for this course. Radio was considered but the idea was not pursued. The course therefore consisted of a series of printed modules which were backed by two-day meetings of heads organised on a district basis.

During the design phase there was discussion of the possibility of using more sophisticated technologies and, indeed, to develop their use within education. At the same time there was considerable scepticism about the new technologies from some countries of the region which were unhappy with earlier experiences. Some of the new technologies were used to help the process of course development and to enable those working on the course nationally and internationally to keep in touch. Thus e-mail was used to keep course designers in touch with each other within Burkina Faso and a CD-ROM of materials was developed for them. RESAFAD used Listserv and Web links were used to keep in touch with its collaborators.

Funding and costs

The programme was funded within the framework of a bilateral aid agreement between Burkina Faso and France. Head teachers were not required to pay a fee and received a per diem allowance when they attended face-to-face sessions. The course was developed in close cooperation with the ministry of basic education and literacy and used resources within the national education system as well as external funds by, for example, drawing on staff time and expertise from teachers' colleges. But the reliance on external funding meant that the project was fragile. Funding came to an end in 2000 and, although it had by then reached only about a quarter of the total number of head teachers, it was not possible to continue it for a further period. A full costing of the course is not available but indicative figures suggest that the costs of any face-to-face alternative would have been significantly greater than that of the distance education version, as well as requiring head teachers to take time away from their schools in order to do so.

Quality, effectiveness and outcomes

The programme was not formally evaluated. It reached 70 head-teachers, within two districts of one region of Burkina Faso in the first, trial year; 920 heads in 30 districts of three regions in the second year and 1,275 heads when it reached 34 districts in four regions in the third year. A total of 1,275 head teachers participated over the three years though within this number some may have participated twice if posted to another district. Most of the heads enrolled were men, varying from 98 per cent of total enrolments in the northern region to 72 per cent in the central region. Very few dropped out of the course which suggests that participants valued it. Head-teachers who had gone through the programme reported favourably on it, identifying ways in which it had resulted in changes in ways in which they managed their schools, and that it had increased their confidence in their work. They had valued the opportunity of face-to-face meetings to share experiences and broaden their understanding of the ground covered by the programme. There is some evidence from reports of school inspectors of more efficient school management as a consequence of the course.

The programme also had some side benefits, in developing national capacity in distance education, including the writing of materials, and in promoting international cooperation in this area. In the last analysis, however, despite the varied evidence of success the programme was not seen as having sufficient priority for its continuation to be funded from national resources.

TEACHERS' LEARNING TO USE INFORMATION TECHNOLOGY, CHILE

This in-service programme enables teachers to learn to use information and communications technology (ICT) in their teaching. It uses ICT to teach teachers to use ICT. Distance education, though fairly new to Chile, was chosen in order to extend the geographical reach of the programme and to meet the teachers' needs for new skills and knowledge created by the recent widespread provision of computers to schools.

The context

The children's education system is undergoing a major reform, with a shift of emphasis from teaching to learning, changes in the curriculum, and moves towards decentralisation. With an advanced communications infrastructure, the country has equipped all of its secondary schools, and about half of its primary schools, with computers under its Enlaces project. This in turn has created a demand for teacher in-service programmes in the use of information technology. There are about seven face-to-face programmes on information technology available for teachers in Chile and one distance education programme offered by the Instituto de Informatica Educativa of the Universidad de la Frontera, an independent public university.

The programme

This programme is designed mainly for primary and secondary school teachers interested in learning how to use ICT in their teaching. It has been offered to four cohorts of students so far with annual enrolments of about 100 students a year each year from 1997 to 2000. About a quarter of the students have been from primary school, nearly a half from secondary schools and the rest from other professions. In the group starting in 2000, about a quarter of students were from outside Chile and one special programme has been run for students from Colombia. The programme consists of seven modules, on education and on the application of communication technologies, and a project, requiring 1,068 hours of study on the part of the students over a period of 15 months. Satisfactory completion of the programme leads to the award of a diploma from the Universidad de La Frontera. Though valued by employers the diploma does not earn a title or lead towards a further degree qualification.

Chile		
Population (millions)		15.0
Size ('000 km²)		757
GDP per capita (purchasing power parity US$)		8,652
Human development index		0.825
Educational data	*Primary*	*Secondary*
Teaching force total '000	73,960	51,042[a]
'000 female	53,593	26,762[a]
Gross enrolment ratio		
All students	101	75
Female	100	78
Pupil teacher ratio	30	–

Source: UNDP 2001; UNESCO 2000; UNESCO 2001

Note: Population, size, GDP and HDI figures are for 1999; Education figures are 1996

Media and technology

The course is entirely computer-based. The institute chose this approach in order to reach a new audience of teachers who could not attend its face-to-face courses, for which demand was failing within the university's locality. It was influenced, too, by the provision of computers and Internet connections to schools through the Enlaces project. Teaching materials were developed by a team of instructional staff at the institute. Students obtain their teaching materials by downloading them from the Web. Their interaction with tutors and with other students is through 'Learning Space' software which replaced an earlier 'homemade' learning environment. In the last phase of the course students develop a collaborative project on the use of ICT in school. They have six months to plan and implement it. Their project proposal is reviewed by teaching staff of the institute and a mid-term and final project report is assessed by one of the institute staff and an external assessor. Some students reported that they would have welcomed opportunities for face-to-face contact but over 80 per cent reported favourably on their computer-based interaction with tutors.

Funding and costs

The programme is funded entirely by student fees. The programme fee is US $860 which is about 10 per cent of the average student income. It includes costs for Internet access but in addition students spend about US $15 per month on telephone charges. Some teachers gain an increment of about 3 per cent of salary on completing the programme. One problem in funding is the difficulty in getting students to pay their fees and a significant proportion of fees remain unpaid: improvements are needed in the system for their collection. The average cost per student of this programme and its face-to-face equivalent were about the same although the breakdown of expenditure was different. About 75 per cent of the costs of the Web-based version of the programme were fixed, with about 40 per cent being used for the work of the instructional teams who were developing the courses. Since the teams used existing print materials from the face-to-face programme, adapting them for Web use, the course development costs were fairly modest. The remaining 25 per cent of costs covered tutorial work, reproduction costs and software licences. Thus there would be considerable scope to achieve economies if it were possible to increase the enrolment in the programme from its present modest levels.

Quality, effectiveness and outcomes

The programme has a good reputation, in part because of the status of the university which provides it and is responsible for quality assurance. Formal measures are in place to check the quality of the teaching materials as they are developed. Generally the fact that the programme is an exact parallel to a conventional, face-to-face one, demanding the same workload and credits and taught by the same instructors, is seen as a guarantee of quality. Completion and graduation rates are available for two cohorts of students. Of the total 169 students who enrolled in 1998 and 1999 (51.5 per cent) dropped out, 7 (4.1 per cent) failed and 75 (44.4 per cent) graduated. There is some evidence that head teachers and students felt that the programme was rewarding and useful: almost all the teachers interviewed by the researchers reported favourably on what they had gained from the programme. In one respect the distance education programme was more effective than its face-to-face equivalent. Teachers participating in it made more use of the virtual working environment than those on the face-to-face programme and developed a 'network communication culture' through their constant use of it. Because of this there was better integration of theory with practice. However, there is little information on how much and how effectively teachers have used ICT in their teaching as a result of the programme.

Reaching Teachers Through Television, China

This case describes the provision of large-scale teacher education through a national distance teaching institution, the China Television Teachers College (CTVTC), a part of the China Central Radio and Television University (CCRTVU) since 1994. Distance education is included in China's strategic planning for teacher education and plays a significant role in initial teacher education and continuing professional development.

The context

China has about 1,100 institutions for pre-service teacher education and 2,000 for in-service (universities, colleges and secondary level training schools). Distance education is an established part of the provision through a number of specialised institutions as well as departments of conventional ones. Much of the provision is aimed at enabling unqualified serving teachers to gain initial qualifications or qualified teachers to upgrade. Though China has made huge strides towards a qualified teaching force and raised minimum qualification standards, all teachers are not yet qualified. About a million (11 per cent of all primary and secondary teachers in 1998, many in rural areas) lack initial qualifications and training. In addition, to improve quality, the government's 'Gardeners' Promotion Project Across the Centuries' (a component in the 'Action Scheme for Invigorating Education Towards the 21st Century') states an ambitious goal of providing 240 hours of non-degree in-service training, including computer literacy, to all kindergarten, primary and secondary teachers in most regions over three years. Altogether, these represent a considerable range and volume of teacher training needs and the Ministry of Education has emphasised a strong role for open and distance learning in meeting them.

The programmes

The China Television Teachers' College (CTVTC) provides a range of distance education programme for serving primary and secondary teachers, school principals and administrators. CTVTC is part of China Central Radio and Television University (CCRTVU), the apex institution of a nation-wide system of 44 Provincial Radio and Television Universities (PRTVUs). CTVTC is in charge of the compulsory (60 per cent) core courses in teacher education programmes; these have a unified syllabus, materials, time-table and assessment methods throughout China. PRTVUs

China		
Population		1,264.8
Size ('000 km²)		9,597[a]
GDP per capita (purchasing power parity US$)		3,617
Human development index		0.718
Educational data	*Primary*	*Secondary*
Teaching force total '000	5,735,790	4,217,947
'000 female	2,718,842	1,537,605
Gross enrolment ratio		
All students	123	70
Female	123	66
Pupil teacher ratio	24	17

Source: UNDP 2001; UNESCO 2000; UNESCO 2001

Notes: Population, size, GDP, and HDI figures are for 1999; Education figures are 1996; a: Figure includes Taiwan, China

are responsible for learner support and local organisation (enrolling students and putting into practice the teacher training plans set by CTVTC). Award-bearing programmes lead to initial and further qualifications (diplomas and, since 1999, degrees). There are also continuing education programmes (non-award-bearing) through television series (for example, 'Friends of Primary School Teachers') with an estimated viewing audience of two million teachers a year.

Media and technology

The main teaching medium is television. Through the use of satellite technology, most areas of China can receive television. China has over 100 educational television channels operating at national and regional levels. CCRTVU transmits its programmes through China Central TV and China Education TV (about 9,000 hours per year). CTVTC programmes are part of these. Through CETV-3 (Channel 3 of China Education TV, dedicated to basic education), CTVTC provides 750 hours a year of continuing education programmes for teachers and school principals. Video-cassette recordings of television programmes are made at local levels (district and county) for use in face-to-face classes or meetings at local centres. Face-to-face meetings are held at local study centres for registered students on award-bearing programmes. Some related printed materials are available, often in the form of regular textbooks. Audio-cassettes are used to a lesser extent and radio very little. Recently, some multi-media packages have been developed (print, audio and video-cassettes). The government has also begun to implement national plans for the provision of ICT-based distance education and 31 universities have been granted licences by the Ministry of Education to offer online programmes, CTVTC will follow this trend as CCRTVU develops greater ICT use in the future, in line with ministry and government policy.

Funding and costs

Detailed information on funding and costs was not available. In general, the total public expenditure per student at China's RTVUs is about one-tenth that of students on conventional programmes. The annual cost per graduate of RTVUs is said to be one-third to two-fifths that of graduates from conventional institutions. Students pay tuition fees for award-bearing programmes. Fees for an RTVU college diploma programme are US $399-544 (an annual average of US $133-181). Tuition fees for a Bachelor's programme for students who already have a college diploma are US $604-725 (with an average of US $40-48 per course).

Quality, effectiveness and outcomes

Quality tends to be judged on the numbers of qualified teachers produced and the reputation of academics and presenters. The television presenters and textbook writers were all well-known professors and scholars in teacher education in China and this was taken as an indicator of the quality of the courses.

Annual figures for enrolment and completion rates were not available, but some cumulative figures were. Between 1987 and 1999, 717,300 unqualified primary teachers gained certificates (the award for secondary school level teacher training) through CTVTC and became qualified for primary teaching, and 552,000 unqualified secondary school teachers (mostly junior-secondary) gained diplomas. A new trial programme ('Open Entrance Programme') was begun in 1997 to upgrade qualified primary teachers from certificate to diploma level. This allowed teachers to enrol for the programme without taking the customary entrance examinations and giving longer to complete (8 years). For this, the diploma examinations are set and assessed by the Self-Taught Examinations Office (an independent examination body under the Ministry of Education) while CTVTC provide the programmes. Upto 1999, 85,000 teachers were enrolled. In 1999, a second new programme (and CCRTVU's first degree programme) was begun ('Pilot Programme of Open Education'), offering degrees and diplomas, similar to the 'Open Entrance Programme' but differing from it in locating control over assessment with CCRTVU. As part of this venture, CTVTC began in 1999 to offer a programme in educational management leading to a college-level higher diploma for primary school principals and administrators. By April 2001, 29,000 students were registered for this programme. Finally, the continuing education series of television programmes and estimated to reach two million teachers annually.

Though efficiency, cost-effectiveness and quality are difficult to judge on the limited data available, there is wide acceptance in China that, without the distance education programme, numbers of teachers and school principals, especially in rural areas, would not have been able to qualify as teachers, or upgrade their qualifications, or have access to continuing education programme.

Developing Primary Teachers' Knowledge and Skills in Child Guidance, India

This case describes a programme in Child Guidance for primary teachers, parents and social workers, provided by the Indira Gandhi National Open University (IGNOU) in India. Using printed text, audio and video materials it provides a practically-oriented non-specialist programme which is not otherwise available. The numbers of students have been relatively small (less than a thousand per year).

The context

Though the study of child development and guidance has become a low priority subject in education in India, the need for it is increasingly recognised by teachers and parents. It is included in teacher education pre-service programmes and a small number of post-graduate ones of a theoretical nature, but easily accessible, basic level programmes of a practical nature were lacking. A perceived need for one by individual staff at the National Council of Educational Research and Training (NCERT) and some parent-teacher associations led to the development of the Certificate in Guidance. This was produced through a collaboration between NCERT and the Indira Gandhi National Open University (IGNOU), the apex distance teaching university in India. NCERT developed the curriculum, content and materials, first in English, then in Hindi, and IGNOU ran the programme.

The programme

The Certificate in Guidance Programme aims to extend understanding about child development (ages 5-11) and to suggest practical strategies to facilitate children's all-round development. It takes about 480 hours of study over six months but students can extend this to two years. The four constituent courses are provided to two languages. Hindi and English (a limitation for speakers of other Indian languages). Printed materials (nine booklets) are supplemented by five audio-cassettes and four video-cassettes. Twelve optional face-to-face tutor-led meetings are provided at weekends at local study centres. Students complete two assignments of a practical nature per course (a total of eight) and sit an examination. On successful completion they are awarded a Certificate in Guidance by IGNOU.

India		
Population (millions)		992.7
Size ('000 km²)		3,288
GDP per capita (purchasing power parity US$)		2,248
Human development index		0.571
Educational data	*Primary*	*Secondary*
Teaching force total '000 '000 female	1,789,733 584,953	– –
Gross enrolment ratio		
All students	100	49
Female	90	39
Pupil-teacher also	47	33

Source: UNDP 2001; UNESCO 2000; UNESCO 2001

Note: Population, size, GDP, and HDI figures are for 1999; Education figures are 1996

Media and technology

IGNOU is equipped to use a variety of media and technology (radio and television, audio-teleconferencing, audio and video-cassettes, phone-in radio programmes, and print). However, for the Certificate in Guidance programme, appropriate technology choices were print, audio and video-cassettes (low cost to produce and use, accessible by students). Print materials were the main medium for the programme and, for some students, the only one they used. Print alone was available in the early years of the programme and audio- and video-cassettes were added later as supplementary material. The video-cassettes are available at local study centres for viewing there, usually during the tutor-led sessions. In practice, a low level of use of audio and video materials is reported, mainly because of low student attendance at study-centre sessions. The materials have had no revision since their production in 1993 and some students have found the level of language difficult.

Funding and costs

The development costs of print (borne by NCERT) are estimated to be US $10,000 in 1993. Programme delivery (including print costs, tutorial support, distribution, examinations and administration) is funded by IGNOU. The certificate programme is a small half-year programme out of a total of about 50 larger and longer programmes provided by IGNOU and cost data on it is limited and difficult to disentangle from other IGNOU programmes and services. The cost per successful student is not available but the total cost per enrolled student is about US $76. The costs of learning materials per enrolled student are about US $3 for printing the booklets, US $10 for developing them, and US $4 for the set of audio and video materials. Teaching costs (tutoring and study centre facilities) are US $36. Because of the low numbers, the Certificate programme costs more per student in teaching costs than other IGNOU programmes. Fees charged to students are Rs. 500 (the equivalent of US $16 in 1993 and US $10 in 2001). Other costs borne by students are between US $12 and US $24, an affordable sum for primary teachers (whose salary is around US $1,800 a year) or for middle-class mothers but not for those with lower incomes. Like other short-term updating or refresher programmes for teachers, the Certificate does not attract any financial increment to a teacher's salary.

Quality, effectiveness and outcomes

The programme is regarded by the providers (NCERT and IGNOU) as a good one, with high quality curriculum, assignment design and printed materials (purchased by those outside the programme too). It has been able to take advantage of its location in a large distance teaching university and the services and resources that this can offer. The providers see the programme as serving a useful social purpose and meeting needs otherwise neglected. However, they are also concerned at the relatively small numbers enrolling (less than a thousand each year) and how completion rates. Between 1993 and 2001 a total of 6,546 students are enrolled for the programme (an average of about 700 students a year). Of the 5,659 students enrolling between 1993 and 2000, 887 (15.7 per cent) have successfully completed it. One reason for this appears to be the heavy study demands of the programme which is constrained by the assessment requirements of a credited course. The question of whether or not a course of this kind should be examined and accredited has been debated by the providers. Other reasons identified include weaknesses in the learner support provided, a need for simpler language in the study materials and speedier feedback to students on their written work, and the heavy workload involved. No evaluation has been done of the impact of the programme on teachers' work in schools. The programme has attracted more women than men; 68 per cent female and 32 per cent male for students enrolling 1999-2001; 15 per cent of students come from deprived sections of society (according to the Government's classification; 50 per cent of places in educational institutions are reserved for deprived sections as affirmative action).

ReOrienting Primary Teachers to New Teaching Approaches, Mongolia

This case describes a project for primary teachers in Mongolia at a time of rapid change and reduced resources for education. Though new to the country, distance education was chosen as an affordable means of teaching more teachers more quickly more often than traditional provision, to reorient them to new teaching approaches and curricula.

The context

During the 1990s, Mongolia made the transition from a single-party socialist state and command economy to a multi-party democracy and market economy. This had a major impact on the education system. It resulted in new curricula, new teaching approaches and examinations, an inflow of ideas from other countries, reduced finances for education, a scarcity of information and learning materials for teachers, and the decentralisation of budgets and decision-making to the provincial level. Primary teachers were qualified but needed in-service development for a changing environment. The traditional in-service model of residential summer courses in the capital city, Ulaanbaatar, was no longer affordable or even appropriate, given the need for the rapid reorientation of all teachers. A different approach was needed, one which could reach more teachers more quickly more often. Distance education was chosen as a means of doing this despite the challenges presented by the country's size, weak communications infrastructure and unfamiliarity with distance education.

The project

The project (1994-2001) was funded by UNICEF in partnership with the Ministry of Science, Technology Education and Culture (MOSTEC) and implemented by the National Institute for In-service Teacher Education, the School of Educational Development (SED). Its aim was to help primary teachers adapt to changes in curriculum, pedagogy and management of learning in primary classes (Grades 1-4 for children from 8-12 years of age). Learning materials (mainly print and radio) were developed to provide information and guidance for teachers. Content focused on integrated subject-teaching, multi-grade and child-centred teaching, and active learning methods. Workshops were organised in provinces, regions and Ulaanbaatar. This was not a structured formal course with assessment and accreditation but had more of the characteristics of open learning, where learning resources are provided and teachers make choices about how they will use them.

Mongolia		
Population (millions)		2.5
Size ('000 km²)		1,567
GDP per capita (purchasing power parity US $)		1,711
Human development index		0.569
Educational data	*Primary*	*Secondary*
Teaching force total '000	7,587	13,171
'000 female	6,812	8,686
Gross enrolment ratio		
All students	88	56
Female	91	65
Pupil teacher ratio	31	15

Source: UNDP 2001; UNESCO 2000; UNESCO 2001

Note: Population size, GDP, and HDI figures are for 1999; Education figures are 1996

Media and technology

The main media were printed materials and audio (radio and audio-cassettes) with a limited amount of video. Print was chosen because it was accessible, affordable, familiar and provided a permanent resource that several teachers could use. Radio was widely accessible through national and provincial radio stations and was affordable too. Programmes were made and transmitted at the national level by Mongol Radio and additional ones by provincial radio stations. Audio-cassette recordings of radio programmes were distributed on request and schools provided with equipment to make their own recordings. Television was available in population centres but development and transmission costs were high and access restricted. Five television programmes were made in 1998, four of them using content coming from teachers and schools. Video-tapes of these were distributed but access to video-cassette players was limited. Computers did not play a role because they are still scarce in most areas of the country and electricity supplies not always reliable or available; connectivity is limited and expensive. The media choices were shaped by four factors: their purpose (for example, telling, showing, illustrating through examples or motivating teachers), accessibility, development and delivery costs and infrastructural constraints. New kinds of uses were made of familiar media and existing technology. Teachers use the print most often and then audio.

Funding and Costs

The main funding (about US $30,000 most years, US $60,000 in two of them) came from UNICEF though the salaries and institutional costs of staff taking part were carried by MOSTEC who collaborated closely. Work was carried out by staff already in post at SED and provincial education centres. There was no charge to teachers. The project's records for managing and auditing project finances do not allow much analysis of the costs of the distance education project. They were kept for a different purpose. It was also impossible to estimate the costs of people's time, especially in retrospect, where activities for this project were only part of their work or coincidental with it. However, some costs can be identified. The development and transmission costs of one 20-minute national radio programme with one repeat transmission was US $110 (estimated costs of content preparation: US $30; production and transmission costs US $80). Printed booklets were produced for about US $1 a copy.

Quality, effectiveness and outcomes

The project introduced a new approach to in-service teacher education. Materials were constructed with the input of teachers and methodologies and capacity built in operating distance education. The printed materials still have some way to go in achieving good quality as self-study materials and provide too small a resource so far but they represent an important beginning. Further development is needed with some technical assistance: the project had little and limitations in materials and strategic planning resulted, since distance education was unfamiliar.

Since there was no structured course or assessment, there are no completion and graduation rates to report. Over 5,000 primary teachers took part in project activities (and still more used the radio and print resources) though the extent of their participation is not known. There is no systematic data on the project's impact on teaching methods but plenty of anecdotal evidence and informal report and examples in schools around the country. The 'UNICEF Project' is well-known in the country though it lacked a clear project title and is well-regarded by teachers.

The project began in four provinces and Ulaanbaatar in 1994 and by 2000 had reached over half of the country's primary teachers. The current funding for the traditional in-service model is only sufficient to provide a teacher with a one-week residential course every ten years. What the project demonstrated was a new way of using limited resources. Whereas the traditional model spent 85 per cent of its budget on travel costs and accommodation the distance education approach spent a much greater proportion on the provision of learning resources and workshop activities.

An Alternative Route to Primary Teacher Qualifications, Nigeria

This case describes the National Certificate in Education (NCE) programme offered by the National Teachers' Institute in Nigeria. It provides an alternative but equivalent route to initial teaching qualifications for working primary teachers in a country very short of qualified teachers and where conventional college output cannot meet demand.

The context

An acute shortage of qualified primary teachers led to the establishment in 1976 of the National Teachers' Institute (NTI), a distance education college for teachers. Its mission was to provide initial teacher qualifications and upgrade the quality of teachers through distance education. Its courses and qualifications were equivalent to those of conventional teachers' colleges. NTI is a parastatal organisation, with headquarters in Kaduna and offices in 36 states. It has made a significant contribution to teacher supply (48,204 NCE graduates between 1990-1999) and is now an institutionalised part of the teacher education system. Though there is little government policy on distance education and no ministry section with overall responsibility for it, distance education has played an enduring role in Nigeria's teacher education and, to meet EFA targets, is likely to do so in the future.

The programme

The NCE programme leads to the national standard qualification for primary teachers. It combines printed self-study materials, tutorials, field trips and supervised teaching practice over four years (the college-based equivalent takes three years). The curriculum covers general (50 modules) and specialist (36) academic subjects, education (36), communication and the use of English (4), field trips and four weeks of supervised teaching practice each year. Learner support is provided at weekends and in school vacations in 220 study centres around the country. Students attend them for tutorials, revision and examination sessions. Supervision of practical teaching in schools is carried out by educators from local higher education institutions who visit students three times during each four-week period and assess them against standardised performance-based assessment criteria. Continuous assessment, tests and practicals constitute 40 per cent of the final grade, examinations for 60 per cent. Teaching practice is compulsory but to qualify for it, students have to attain a grade of 60 per cent in coursework.

Nigeria		
Population (millions)		110.8
Size ('000 km²)		924
GDP per capita (purchasing power parity US $)		853
Human development index		0.455
Educational data	*Primary*	*Secondary*
Teaching force		
total '000	435,210[a]	152,596[a]
'000 female	201,905[a]	54,596[a]
Gross enrolment ratio		
All students	98	33
Female	87	30
Pupil teacher ratio	37	–

Source: UNDP 2000; UNESCO 2000; UNESCO 2001

Note: Population size, GDP and HDI figures are for 1999; Education figures are 1996; a: 1994

Media and technology

The NCF programme is print-based. Supplementary audio and video-cassette materials are produced for use in study centres. Study centres are intended to serve as access points to telephone, radio and television, newsletters and mini-libraries but, in practice, most study centres are devoid of these facilities and resources. Given the country's infrastructure and resources levels, the choice of media and technologies is limited.

Funding and costs

NTI is funded directly by the Federal Ministry of Education. It generates some income through its printing press, publishing, resource and conference centre. Students buy their own course materials at the study centres or state NTI office but even these relatively low costs to students are not always easily affordable: recent teachers' strikes and slow salary payments by the government have affected trainees' ability to pay and may account for some drop-outs.

Limited data is available on costs but the evidence suggests that of 5,167 students completing in 1999, 2,872 passed the examination at a unit cost of US $203 while the other 2,295 graduated, after retakes, at a unit cost of US $259. This produces an average cost per graduate of US $ 228 which includes loss through drop-out. This compares with a unit cost per graduate in a regular college of education of US $317 (1998), US $469 (1999) and US $529 (2000).

Quality, effectiveness and outcomes

Accreditation and quality control for all NCE programmes in Nigeria, including the distance one, is undertaken by the National Commission for Colleges of Education (NCCE). This body visits centres, appraises the quality and quantity of tutors and sets the grading and assessment system. Teaching practice and examination scripts are externally moderated. The learning materials are acknowledged to have a value wider than the distance education programme alone and have been used in other West African countries (Sierra Leone, Gambia and Ghana).

The programme has steadily rising enrolment rates: 7,324 (1994-97 cohort), 7,581 (1995-98), 8,398 (1996-99) and 8,521 (1997-2000). However, these are matched by significant drop-out rates: 27 per cent (1994-97 cohort), 30 per cent (1995-98), 35 per cent (1996-99) and 39 per cent (1997-2000). Of those completing this course, only 56.5 per cent passed in the 1994-97 cohort, 66 per cent in 1995-98, 61.4 per cent in 1996-99 and 55.6 per cent in 1997-2000. Several reasons are given for high drop-out rates: the inability of trainees to afford course materials; the time needed for other income-generating activities; the disruption to the studies of female trainees as they follow a re-located husband; the demands of busy farming periods at examination time (especially in the northern states like Sokoto and Kano); late delivery of materials because of poor postal services; long distances to travel to study centres; failure to participate in the practical teaching element (a compulsory part of the course) and low pass rates in assignments and tests. Some problems in the quality of learner support play a role. Study centres are under-resourced and overstretched, dealing with more students than planned for when established; appropriate local tutors are difficult to recruit; and the activities provided at study centres tend to mimic the formal practices of conventional colleges or traditional ways of teaching, eroding the intention of providing opportunities for interaction between learners and learners and tutors.

Despite the problems, the NTI's NCE programme has made a significant numerical impact on teacher supply in Nigeria. Twenty one thousand trainees graduated with the NCE qualification in 1994, a number comparable with the total admissions of the 58 regular colleges of education.

Interactive Radio for Supporting Teachers of English as a Second Language, OLSET, South Africa

The south African radio project has two audiences: primary school children and their teachers. Through a well-structured curriculum and active learning approaches, the children learn English while the teachers improve both their English and their teaching of it.

The context

In 1994 the new post-apartheid government in South Africa faced enormous challenges in redressing great inequalities in education. Wide disparities existed between schools for different ethnic groups in funding, resources, pupil-teacher ratios and teaching qualifications and skills. About 29 per cent of teachers were underqualified and 7 per cent unqualified. Since then the government has created a single unified system of education but schools and teachers till vary in quality. The in-service training of teachers is not well developed. This limits the possibilities for improvements in teacher quality and for implementing the many changes facing them, for example, the policy shift from a content-based to outcomes-based curriculum. The 'English in Action' programme has attempted to address these issues in the context of teaching English as a second language. In South Africa, English is an official language but for many children and teachers, it is their second or third or even fourth language. The project was begun in 1993 and is run by a non-governmental organisation, the Open Learning System Education Trust (OLSET).

The programme

'English in Action' is an interactive radio programme series. 'Interactive radio' is an approach used in several countries. It designs radio lessons to structure children's and teachers' learning activities as the radio lessons proceed, with pauses left for responses and action. In using it for English language teaching, it also provides a good model of pronunciation and language use if teachers have weak spoken English. In the OLSET project, the daily half-hour radio lessons introduce pupils (Grades 1-3 in primary schools) to English through activities such as stories, music and songs. The lessons involve teachers as partners in the teaching process by asking them to lead language development activities, such as games or pairwork, and to mediate content, if necessary in the mother tongue. The teachers, who may themselves have low levels of English or poor teaching methods, are supported by a structured and well-planned language curriculum which also introduces them to new teaching practices designed to foster active learning. Teachers are supported by visiting programme coordinators who organise training workshops and teachers' groups as well as supplying equipment and printed visual aids to the schools. From small beginnings in 300 classrooms in 1993-94, the project has grown to involve an estimated 11,000 teachers and 550,000 pupils in nine regions of South Africa in 2001.

South Africa		
Population (millions)		42.8
Size (0'00 km²)		1,221
GDP per capita (purchasing power parity US $)		8,908
Human development index		0.702
Educational data	*Primary*	*Secondary*
Teaching force total '000	224,896[a]	113,215[b]
'000 female	165,398[a]	71,452[b]
Gross enrolment ratio		
All students	133	95
Female	131	103
Pupil-teacher ratio	36	29

Source: UNDP 2001; UNESCO 2000; UNESCO 2001

Note: Population size, GDP, and HDI figures are for 1999; Education figures are 1996; a: 1995; b: 1991

Media and technologies

Radio is the main medium used, supported by printed materials. OLSET supplies participating schools with battery-powered radios and, in certain areas, wind-up or solar-powered ones. The radio lessons are supported by printed materials for pupils and teachers: a teacher's manual, pupil activity workbooks, posters and a comic reading book. The half-hour radio lessons are produced and recorded by OLSET, and are delivered through daily radio broadcasts by the national radio organisation, the South African Broadcasting Corporation (SABC), and some community radio stations. Where reception is difficult or broadcasting schedules unreliable, schools are provided with tape recorders and tapes of the lessons though this has added extra tasks and costs to the project. Negotiation of access and airtime for programme transmissions has been a continual battle and created some problems for the project. Prior to a recent agreement with SABC to broadcast the programme nationally, the radio lessons were broadcast in some areas by SABC radio broadcasts and in others by community radio stations. This led to erratic implementation of the programme in some places and affected the regularity of lesson delivery. The programme has suffered from the lack of consistent policy on educational broadcasting at national and local level.

Funding and costs

OLSET is funded by the United States Agency for International Development, Norwegian Government aid and more recently, by the UK Government's Department for International Development (DfID). While this external funding has sustained the project since 1993, it leaves the project vulnerable to changes in funding policies and priorities as competing needs arise for international donors. The total costs of administration were estimated as US $125,000 in 2001, and the costs of production and distribution US $390,000. On these figures and at the current scale of operation, the cost per child is about US $1 per year. Programme transmission and airtime are provided free of charge by radio stations, including SABC. Where there are problems in receiving the radio programme, audiotapes and cassette-players are provided to schools and this is a more expensive (per capita) option than radio. There are no costs to teachers or pupils.

Quality, effectiveness and outcomes

The programme has had the benefit of ongoing formative evaluation from its inception in 1993 and is well-documented. After early positive evaluation findings in both urban and rural schools, the programme grew rapidly. By mid-2001 it was estimated that 'English in Action' was used in 11,000 primary school classrooms and that 55,000 pupils were regularly exposed to the radio broadcasts. Government education officials are said to endorse widely the project's practical, performance-based approach. There has also been firm support for the programme from teachers and school principals. This appears to confirm their (otherwise unmet) needs for in-service training and support and for practical assistance in planning and teaching a subject in which some of them have low levels of competence. There is a strong demand for the OLSET printed materials as well as for the OLSET radios, which are commonly used teaching aids in many South African primary schools. Pupils appear to be well motivated by the radio lessons and there is some evidence of learning gains in the use of English. Other evidence suggests that teachers, as second-language speakers of English themselves, have gained confidence in teaching English and are able to use the programmes effectively and to link what is taught in them to other areas of the curriculum.

So far, the project has worked with minimal staff and focused its resource on broadcasting to the maximum number of pupils and teachers. Its rapid growth has sometimes outstripped resources, resulting in problems in the quality of regional support and competing demands on scarce staff time. Expansion has greatly increased administrative demands without an accompanying increase in staffing. However, with the agreement by the SABC to provide airspace for the programme nationally, and with promises of increased funding from the international donor community, the project hopes to increase its scale even further. To achieve this, the project will need to employ additional staff and develop a more substantial administrative and regional infrastructure. More formal systems of evaluation and quality control will also be necessary. OLSET is also working with the British Broadcasting Corporation to share teachers' experiences of working with interactive radio with other teachers in the developing world.

New Routes to Teacher Education Degrees, South Africa

This case describes degree programmes in teacher education provided by the University of South Africa (UNISA), one of the world's largest distance teaching universities. Distance education plays a prominent role in teacher education in South Africa—more than a third of its primary and secondary teachers were involved in distance education in 1995. The programmes in this case began as in-service ones but later diversified to include a pre-service target group too, in response to government policy change.

The context

UNISA has been a major provider of distance education and teacher education at tertiary level throughout the southern African region from the 1940s. It has a well-established centre and structure. The main campus is in Pretoria with regional offices in Cape Town, Durban and Pietersburg. In the early 1980s and 1990s UNISA's main role in teacher education was to provide upgrading programmes for serving primary and secondary teachers at the diploma and graduate levels. From the mid-1990s, UNISA has undergone a period of change in attempting to respond to new national priorities in teacher education and to improve the quality of some of its services (such as learner support). One response by the university has been to offer its teacher education programmes to a more diverse audience. The two programmes here, for primary and secondary teachers, have provided a means for non-graduate serving teachers to gain a teacher education degree equivalent to those offered by conventional universities. Until recently, UNISA offered mainly in-service teacher education but has diversified into pre-service initial teacher education through offering the same programme to both target groups of students. These will shortly be revised as South Africa moves towards a standardisation of teacher qualifications.

The programme

Since 1998, UNISA has offered two teacher education programmes at bachelor's degree level, for primary and secondary teachers (BPrimED and BSecEd). These can be taken as in-service or pre-service programmes by students with appropriate levels of entry qualifications. They combine printed self-study materials, assignments, discussion classes and supervised teaching practice over four years (480 credits in total, 120 required credits and 1,200 notional hours of participation per year). The curriculum in each programme has three components: Educational themes (pedagogy), professional studies and selected areas of specialisation or school subjects. There are five weeks of teaching practice annually (20 weeks over the four-year programme). Pre-service students are responsible for arranging their teaching practice in schools of their choice and are supervised by senior teachers there. Supervising teachers assess students' practice according to criteria provided by UNISA and report to the UNISA organiser. Students attend the main campus in Pretoria twice a year for assignment and examination orientation and examinations are held at one of 442 examination centres around the country. Course assignments are normally compulsory and a condition of entrance to the examinations, though do not contribute to the final grade.

South Africa		
Population (millions)		42.8
Size ('000 km²)		1,221
GDP per capita (purchasing power parity US $)		8,908
Human development index		0.702
Educational data	*Primary*	*Secondary*
Teaching force total '000	224,896[a]	113,215[b]
'000 female	165,398[a]	71,452[b]
Gross enrolment ratio		
All students	133	95
Female	131	103
Pupil-teacher ratio	36	29

Source: UNDP 2001; UNESCO 2000; UNESCO 2001

Note: Population size, GDP, and HDI figures are for 1999; Education figures are 1996; a: 1995; b: 1991

Media and technologies

The main medium used is print. On registration, each student receives a print 'tutorial package' containing a tutorial letter, self-study materials (known as study guides), information on prescribed texts (not included) and some audio and video tapes where applicable. In most cases the study guides are designed as 'wrap-around' guides to the textbooks or tutorial materials. UNISA maintains contact with students through regular tutorial letters (six per year). These provide guidance on assignments and examinations (including past papers), tutor contact names and venues for forthcoming discussion classes. Study guides contain compulsory units and also refer the student to selected parts of accompanying textbooks. These print materials are supplemented by face-to-face contact sessions (discussion classes), practical work and some on-line learning activities. UNISA is in the process of integrating Computer Mediated Communication (CMC) and World Wide Web (WWW) technologies into their programmes and this is expected to grow. However, the print-based delivery mode continues at present, with varying optional amounts of on-line use, playing a small optional role in these teacher education programme.

Funding and costs

It was estimated (in 2000) that each of the programme modules of the programme had been developed at a total cost of approximately US $26,078. The number of students enrolled for each module has varied, with a unit cost per student of between US $1,222 per module (where only two students had enrolled for a module) to just over US $9 where the enrolment per module was 259 students. The average delivery cost per student per module was estimated at US $30. All formal teacher education programmes are state-funded so UNISA received grants for these programmes.

Student fees for each individual module (in 2000) were US $67. Given that each qualification comprises 40 modules, the total cost to a student for a complete bachelor's programme is about US $2,682. Similar modules at residential universities are around US $128 each.

Quality, effectiveness and outcomes

Quality assurance measures include the external assessment of courses and modules, the external moderation of question papers and examination scripts. To keep the materials up-to-date, the study guides are revised every three years and reviewed by external assessors. Turn-around of assignments takes three weeks to give students' feedback within a specified time. Quality assurance for teaching practice is provided by the students' workbooks recording their activities and lesson plans and the assessment of teaching practice according to a common set of criteria plus a report by the supervising teacher to UNISA. The differences in the two target audiences, in terms of their teaching experience and the role it plays for them within the programme, raises some issues for the management of the teaching practice of the two groups and the kinds of support materials provided. However, there was no information available on this in the draft materials available for this summary.

The annual pass rates for the individual modules vary between 40 per cent and 65 per cent. Almost 70 per cent UNISA as a whole has experienced an overall drop in enrolments in its programmes and this has limited the amount of funding available to support new initiatives in general and the development of student support in particular. This has been offset to some extent by improvements in government subsidy earned by increased pass rates.

Using ICT to Support School-Based Initial Teacher Education, United Kingdom

This case describes the use of ICT and distance education to support the school-based training of graduates in the United Kingdom. The programme is provided by the Open University, UK and reflects government policy to increase the role of school experience and the use of competency-based approaches in the initial preparation of teachers.

The context

Teaching in the United Kingdom is an all-graduate profession for primary and secondary teachers. In addition, teachers are required to take a recognised training programme leading to qualified teacher status. The programmes take two principal forms: a Bachelor of Education (B.Ed.) with professional training incorporated during the four-year programme, and a one-year full-time Post-graduate Certificate of Education (PGCE) taken by university graduates. In the PGCE, the focus is on education, pedagogy and practical skills since student-teachers already have degrees in academic subjects. In the 1990s, there was a shift in government policy on teacher education, giving a new emphasis to school-based training and the development of teachers' competencies. There was also a growing teacher shortage, especially in mathematics and science, which led to a search for new sources of potential teachers (e.g., women graduates with young families or qualified professionals wanting to change careers). After some research on the need and potential audience for a part-time distance education programme, the government's Department of Education (DES) decided to support one and invited tenders for it. The Open University was successful in winning this and the result was the Open University's PGCE.

The programme

The programme (part-time over eighteen months) led to the same PAGE qualification for primary and secondary teachers as a one-year full-time programme provided by other universities. It was accredited by the Open University and used an assessment framework developed from national regulations. It was planned around three stages of student experience with a period of full-time teaching by students in each. Assessment of learning was based on work produced for a student portfolio and a competency-based assessment of practical skills. There were no written examinations. Part-time tutors and school-based mentors were jointly responsible for the formative and summative assessment of students, with moderation and monitoring by the programme team and external examiners. Teaching practice was supervised and assessed primarily by experienced teachers within an agreed system. ICT played a large role in enabling interaction between students, tutors, regional support centres and programme providers while based in schools. Contracts were made with schools for the services they would provide a payment made for these and materials and training provided for mentors.

Media and technology

A combination of media was used in an integrated way by programme course teams. The materials included specially-designed printed self-study texts, study guides and course readers containing a variety of selected articles; course resource packs for each student, containing print, video-cassettes and audio-cassettes for each course stage. Computer communication between students and students and tutors played a key role, using the Open University's First Class conferencing and e-mail system. All students were provided with a computer and modem for the

United Kingdom		
Population (millions)		59.3
Size ('000 km²)		245
GDP per capita (purchasing power parity US$)		22,093
Human development index		0.923
Educational data	*Primary*	*Secondary*
Teaching force total '000	283,492	464,134
'000 female	228,677	255,669
Gross enrolment ratio		
All students	116	129
Female	116	139
Pupil teacher ratio	19	13

Source: UNDP 2001; UNESCO 2000; UNESCO 2001.

Note: Population, size, GDP and HDI figures are for 1999; Education figures are 1996

duration of the programme to enable them to develop ICT skills, to provide a means of communication while located in schools and to give them access to a range of electronic resources. Competence in the use of ICT is a statutory requirement for newly qualified teachers in the UK. Since many of the Open University PCGE students were older (average age 33) than those on the full-time programme and less familiar with computers, access to computers and support in learning to use them was seen as important.

Funding and costs

The Open University received a government grant of about US $3.5 million (£2.2 million) to develop the programme. It also received US (£6,000 (£3,900) per student in fees and recurrent grants at the outset of the programme; 75 per cent of this was allocated to the PGCE programme and 25 per cent retained by the Open University to cover overheads. Two elements of the costs accounted for 45 per cent of the total cost generated by each student: a payment to schools of US $1,560 (£1,000) per student for their training role, and the cost of computer purchases. These costs are specific to the PGCE programme within the Open University. The cost of an Open University PGCE to the national exchequer is said to be about 50 per cent of a conventional PGCE, though no detailed cost studies were available. All PGCE students in the UK receive a mandatory grant to cover tuition fees but Open University PGCE students do not receive the maintenance (substance) grants paid to full-time PGCE students (about US $ 6,200 or £4,000), a factor in reducing the cost of the distance education programme to government. The initial development costs (for the development of materials and an institutional infrastructure) were not recouped through fees, so any re-development of the programme, without such a grant, would need to take this into account, though could build on the earlier experience.

Quality, effectiveness and outcomes

A strong quality assurance framework was put in place to satisfy three sets of requirements; those of the national body responsible for teacher education (the Teacher Training Agency), those of the Open University for all its programmes, and those created by the need to manage and monitor a complex operation with many players (students, schools, mentors, tutors, head teachers, regional centres). The programme, like those from conventional institutions, was inspected by the responsible government agency who also make the results of all inspections publicly available on their website. The programme and materials were developed with the input of external assessors, as is usual in Open University UK courses, and external examiners were involved in assessing students' work and performance. The materials were of high quality and widely used outside the programme by schools and other training providers.

In 1995-56, 21,000 students entered a full-time PGCE programme in the UK and 14,300 a B.Ed. programme. In the year, the Open University's PGCE enrolled about 1,500 students, just over 7 per cent of the national total. A survey of three cohorts of primary PGCE graduates (1994-96) founded that only 21 students (2 per cent) had not entered teaching (better than the national average). A total of 6,272 students enrolled for the programme during its life but no data was available on completion rates. The programme was particularly successful in recruiting mathematics and science graduates (shortage subjects in the United Kingdom) and there is some evidence that the graduates from the PGCE programme stayed in post longer than younger equivalents from traditional PGCE programmes. In 1999, the Open University withdrew the primary teacher programme because, as a large distance-teaching institution with long preparation times for course production, it could not respond quickly enough to the Teacher Training Agency's new national curriculum for teachers in mathematics, English and computer training.

Conclusions

These ten case studies provide us with a significant body of data to further our understanding about the use of distance education for teacher education. Although the case studies were limited in their scope and took place in only nine countries, they make it possible to draw some conclusions about the appropriate uses of open and distance learning, its effectiveness and costs. The evidence also provides some guidance on key aspects for planners—on technologies, management and funding structures.

As we begin to assess this data, one general observation can be made about most of the studies. They are strong on description but on evaluative data, both quantitative and qualitative, on which to make judgements about effectiveness. The reasons are varied. However, the shortcomings in evaluation data are not only a feature of distance education provision. We should note too that this can also be said of most teacher education provided through conventional pre-service teachers' colleges and in-service provision, including projects for curriculum reform.

In this particular research, the short time-scale of the case studies limited the possibility for much original empirical research. Most researchers were dependent on drawing from existing evaluative literature and data where it existed. More generally, there are also difficulties in researching a complex and interrelated range of factors related to effectiveness. The way that distance education disperses responsibility for a programme among a range of partners, sometimes on a large scale over distance—for student support, administration, tutoring, course production, delivery and assessment—presents a number of logistical and methodological challenges for researchers.

Why is evaluation data so limited? A range of reasons emerges from the particular case studies. In some the generally restricted research capacity of a programme is due to lack of funding, or time, or an education tradition and structure which leaves the evaluation of programmes to another division or institution. In others it results from a lack of a research culture and skills in evaluation. In programmes with a wide geographical reach, data from the centre could not tell us how well it is working at more local levels. Often, the means for gathering data was problematic:

> The main constraint for researching the programme is the lack of an organised database with information about it. Even though the staff was open and willing to help, they did not have an easy way of getting some information and in some cases their memory was the only source available. The teaching unit is now designing a database.
>
> *Cerda, Leon and Ripoll, teachers learning to use information technology, Chile*

It follows, then, the while that data from the case studies advances our understanding it can only be considered as partial. Nonetheless it points us towards those aspects where further research is needed as well as highlighting the practices needed for better management of information and evaluation data. We now turn to examining the data.

What is it being used for?

The case studies show that, as discussed in earlier, distance education is playing a role in four different but sometimes overlapping areas of teacher education: initial professional education, continuing professional development, curriculum reform and changes, and teachers' career development.

Three case studies in three very different countries play a role in *initial teacher education*—the China Television Teachers' College, the National Teachers' Institute in Nigeria, the PGCE programme of the UK Open University. The programmes in China and Nigeria take in large numbers of entrants and make a substantial numerical contribution to increasing qualified teacher supply. In contrast the

British Open University programme makes a contribution towards providing alternative opportunities for trainee teachers but in comparison to the Nigerian and Chinese cases, its numerical impact on UK teacher supply is small. The 1998 figures reveal an intake of 1,933 trainee teachers (224 primary level, 1,709 secondary level) compared with a national annual intake of new teachers of some 30,000. However, there is some evidence from other research that twice as many teachers trained through the UK Open University's PGCE stay in the profession as the national average (up to 40 per cent of newly trained teachers in England leave teaching within three years of qualifying). So while its numerical impact on supply may be small at the point of qualification (less than 7 per cent of all newly-qualified teachers), it may constitute a slightly larger proportion in the longer term in the light of teacher retention rates. This finding is also reported informally in some other countries though empirical evidence is lacking. There has been little study of the employment patterns and careers of teachers, those trained by distance education and by conventional programmes. We need more information on returns over time to investment in teacher education.

The three programmes provide initial training for different levels of learners, for those with secondary-level entry qualifications in China and Nigeria to graduate entry in the United Kingdom. It shows that distance education can accommodate these differences. The programmes also handle the management of teaching practice in different ways, reflecting the regulations and norms of the different countries and the importance placed on it within different teacher education systems. While the whole programme from the UK Open University is designed around school experience, in the China programme it is minor and given little emphasis. In the UK programme, contact with students on teaching practice in schools and a reduction of their isolation—a problem area in all initial teacher education programmes—is facilitated by the employment of ICT. The labour-intensive nature of the management of school practice in the UK, together with the use of ICT and a use of several media in combination is likely to increase the quality of teacher preparation but perhaps at a cost.

Continuing professional development is characterised by a diversification of provision, in terms of types of programmes, duration, management, technology and audience, and is an area in which distance education can play a significant role. Two of the cases (A-Plus in Brazil and the Certificate in Guidance in India) illustrate the range and both include the broader community. The A-plus television programme uses mass media on a large scale to reach a wide community of viewers while at the same time using the series as a launching pad for further activities by groups of teachers. This case illustrates how mass media like television or radio can provide a responsive means of meeting teachers' needs within relatively short timelines. They can be topical, 'of the moment' in ways that are more difficult for print to achieve alone (in combination these two media have the potential to be greater than the sum of the two parts). The Certificate in Guidance has a less wide reach and provides a structured course which shows both the strengths and limitations of centrally-produced print materials; a high quality resource in the eyes of providers but not wholly appropriate from the perspective of users, less easy and slow to up-date by itself. It also illustrates a different approach, bringing the academic context of its location (a university) to bear and demanding a heavy workload from learners—perhaps too heavy to retain their participation. These two cases also have very different funding sources and costs.

Other cases in this set of ten also have a professional development function too, so we would ask readers not to restrict comparisons to these two cases only. For example, some in-service programmes play an upgrading role in countries where individual teachers and government policies are trying to improve the standard of qualification. China and South Africa (UNISA) illustrate this. What emerges overall is the flexibility of open and distance learning in meeting different kinds of needs in a variety of ways, but also the need for planners to make appropriate choices taking a number of factors into account (for example, nature and needs of audience, purposes of provision, function within overall provision for professional development, other options available to teachers, appropriate and affordable media, capacity of providers, the acceptable compromises and trade-offs of different choices.

Curriculum reform and change

Major problems in curriculum reform and change have been informing teachers in time, involving them sufficiently in the change process and supporting them as they change their beliefs and practices either as individuals or groups. This is frequently neglected. Solutions have often resulted in slow information flows, inadequate or scarce support materials and slow, expensive cascades of increasingly diluted information with insufficient support for applying new approaches and practices in teaching. Three cases here showed different approaches in the use of open and distance learning to support change.

The Universidad de la Frontera programme, supporting the teachers involved in the Enlaces project which introduced ICT to schools in Chile, provided an on-line programme for teachers, as an alternative option to face-to-face programmes and ensured that the course assignments were of an applied nature. Though the cost of the two alternatives (face-to-face and on-line) were about the same, the on-line programme appeared to achieve more change, in fostering more familiarity with ICT and the development of a 'network communication culture' missing from the face-to-face vision. The OLSET programme in South Africa has been effective in reaching large numbers of teachers not only with prescription and advice on how to teach English as a second language but with well-designed lessons, provision of models, guidance in using the radio or audio-cassette resources and support for changes in teaching methods. There is some evidence that not only has the programme reached large numbers at low cost, it has been effective in helping young pupils to improve their English and teachers improve their teaching as well as their English. Using radio in a different kind of way, as a topical magazine and involving teachers in topic identification and programme construction, primary teachers in Mongolia became familiar with new ideas about child-centred teaching and other new approaches and were able to apply them to their teaching. The radio programmes were linked to print materials which served a different kind of function. This case showed that open and distance learning could reach more teachers more often more quickly by changing the way the in-service funds were used.

If *continuing* professional development is to have real meaning, it has to provide the opportunities and resources which translate into more than one week per teacher every 10 years. So in terms of scale, variety of purpose and ability to support change, there are some indications that open and distance learning has considerable potential. Of course more research and evaluation are needed. The OLSET programme has benefited from several formative evaluations, using the findings to varying degrees. The Chile and Mongolia cases both rely on informal reports of positive impact on teaching and again point to the need for evaluation to be planned into project activities from the start.

Teachers' career development

One example of career development is given here though teachers may also further their careers through the professional development opportunities described in the other categories. In Burkina Faso, over a quarter of the country's head teachers (whose professional development is increasingly seen as a key element in school effectiveness) developed new knowledge and skills within four years. This served at least three functions: it furthered their careers, but capacity in the head teacher cohort and provided professional development. The upgrading programmes mentioned in this report also serve to further teachers' careers, especially where they are accredited.

How effective is it?

What can we say about effects and effectiveness, completion rates and classroom effectiveness? Some programmes reached large numbers (millions) of teachers and educators, others comparatively small numbers (less than 100) though context plays a role in making these judgements. In the context of India, an annual enrolment of 1,000 for a course is small, in some other countries this would be large. In general, we can conclude that distance education can reach more teachers than conventional programmes and where mass media are involved, can reach very large numbers. The numbers reached by the one wholly on-line programme (in Chile) were relatively small and while this form has the capacity to expand, we have little information on the cost implications of the addition of more tutors or staff for expanded numbers or the comparative workloads involved.

Reaching teachers is one thing, generating teacher activity and application of ideas and knowledge to teaching and schools as an outcome is another. The case of Brazil showed how the reach of mass media could be partnered with support for local action to achieve the best of both worlds. In China, delivery appears as the main goal (again using mass media to reach large numbers) and the mobilisation of recipients less emphasised. This may reflect different cultural perspectives on the roles of learners and the balance between supply and demand in providing training and professional development. The reach of programmes cannot be considered in isolation from time-span. Some cases, such as Mongolia, showed that distance education was able to reach more teachers more quickly than traditional alternatives. There it reached over half of the country's primary teachers, and so had the potential to influence the rate of change of teachers' or head teachers' beliefs and practices within schools. This too could be seen in OLSET. South Africa, where the programme reached over half a million pupils and their teachers within eight years and there is evidence of its positive impact. The programme in Burkina Faso reached a quarter of the country's head teachers so affected a significant proportion of them. There is another sense in which distance education has 'reach'. It was used to reach new constituencies of potential teachers who would otherwise not have entered teaching (the case of the UK Open University illustrates this) or received in-service development or support for teaching (as the cases of OLSET, Mongolia and Burkina Faso show).

We can say a little about completion rates but not much. The case study researchers were not always able to obtain the information (at times it was not clear if the providing organisations themselves knew them or were simply reluctant to reveal them). Also, some provision was not in the form of formal courses but more like open learning where teachers participated as and when they chose. It was difficult too to get programme completion rates for the conventional system for comparison. For the formal distance education programmes, completion rates varied widely. In Burkina Faso, very few head teachers dropped out, in Chile's ICT programme 51 per cent failed to complete, mainly because of problems with fee payment. In the case of Nigeria, drop-out rates varied from 27-39 per cent and the pass rates of those completing the programme varied from 55 per cent to 64 per cent. These indicate some inefficiencies in the system or flaws in programme design since these drop-out rates are high in relation to the average rate for other distance education programmes. In the Certificate in Guidance (India), the completion rate was about 15 per cent suggesting, the need for major review. In the UK Open University case, completion rates appeared to be relatively high but no specific information on them was available to the researchers.

Overall, the main reasons identified for drop-out were fee-problems, heavy and sometimes inappropriate workload, operational failures or weak management in the distance education system and, very importantly, weak learner support systems. For teachers, tangible rewards at the end of programmes play a role too. Generally, experience and research show that drop-out from distance education programmes tends to be higher than for traditional alternatives (though recent studies of conventional programmes at higher-education level indicates that the gap is much less than previously thought and, in some cases, is comparable).

In some of the cases [(China, Nigeria, South Africa (OLSET)] distance education for teachers is a significant part of the system and a part of national strategic planning for teacher supply and upgrading quality. In others, it has provided an alternative (Chile, United Kingdom) or supplement (Brazil, India). In some countries it has filled a gap that would otherwise have continued unfilled (Mongolia, Burkina Faso) and has introduced innovatory approaches, more appreciated by governments in some countries (Mongolia) than others (Burnika Faso) as a possible productive strategy to support. In general, policy-makers need to consider more often the option of distance education as a way of providing initial and continuing professional development but to do this well they need more information on its potential outcomes, strengths, limitations constraints, media choices, costs and operational and policy requirements. While some of this information is available, much is still not because of weaknesses in the research and evaluation base and inadequate dissemination of existing information. Mistakes get repeated or opportunities missed because planners are not always well-informed.

One focus of concern in all teachers education programmes whether distance education or conventional, is to turn what teachers know and believe into what teachers to support children's learning. Weaknesses in achieving this apply to conventional programmes as well as to distance education ones. Many conventional programmes fail to attend to this and some produce 'qualified teachers' who have had only a token or minimal of supervised school experience. In some countries, practical teaching forms no part of the final assessment of teachers. The issues for a distance education provider are how to manage the supervision and assessment of students in distant locations and how to design materials and activities in ways which integrate knowledge or theory with practice. In these cases we have examples of different strategies: a support structure for local action-groups of teachers (Brazil), delegation of supervision and assessment to school staff, with varying degrees of prescription and support (Nigeria, UK, UNISA South Africa), the provision of teaching content, models and sequenced structure in the lessons provided for children (OLSET South Africa), the design of course-work to require a practical application (Chile and UK), the exchange of practical experience in workshops and newsletters (Mongolia and Brazil) or through websites (Chile and UK), the demonstration of model lessons through television or video (China), the use of applied projects rather than examinations on theory and the inclusion of the assessment of performance in the final grade on formal programmes (Nigeria, UK). Some of the ten cases place the practice of teaching as the central focus in programme design and organisation, other assign it a relatively minor, or even marginal, place, not because of the logistical difficulties involved for a distance education provider but because of the traditions and perceptions of teacher education in the different countries, and its role in conventional teacher education programmes.

In general the strategies to integrate theory with practice in these case studies fall into the three categories identified by Robinson (1997):

- *knowledge about practice* (a teacher is able to explain what multi-grade teaching is and produce an essay or examination answer on it);

- *knowledge applied to practice* (a teacher can plan the organisation of multi-grade teaching or materials for it and show how these might be used in the situation or report and reflect on work done);
- *demonstration of knowledge and understanding through performance* (a teacher shows the use of multi-grade teaching through the conduct of teaching and learning activities, observed by others).

The different categories have different logistical and cost implications for distance education. One danger here is that activities in the first category are (wrongly) assumed by programme providers to result in the outcomes found in the third (competence in performance) as a matter of course. They do not. However, for most of our ten cases, we lack sufficient evidence of the extent to which knowledge gained translated into knowledge applied in fostering children's learning. This lack of evidence is to be found in traditional teacher education too but is an aspect of research and evaluation much needed in distance education programmes, to aid designers and policy-makers.

What does it cost?

The case studies confirm the existing finding that distance education can be at an economic advantage over conventional provision but it is not always so. The reasons for this are to do with scale, choice of media and technology and programme design.

Some lower costs are reported. Initial teacher education in Nigeria by distance education has lower costs than conventional programmes. The UK Open University claims costs to the exchequer are lower than conventional programmes though some of the cost-savings come from the absence of subsistence grants to distance mode students. The ICT on-line programme in Chile cost about the same as its face-to-face equivalent though the cost structure was used differently. The true costs of it were difficult to establish (since some costs were absorbed by the parent institution) and cost-recovery was not possible because the system for collecting students' fees was ineffective.

Some distance education programmes have no traditionally-delivered equivalents for comparison, especially in continuing professional development programmes. What is possible in some cases is to compare differences between similar programmes within the same institution. For example, because of low numbers, the Certificate in Guidance (India) programme had higher student support costs (tutoring and study centre facilities) than other larger-population programmes within the same institutions. Attendance at study centres was low so the services were under-used so it can be argued that the most costly component yielded the least benefit to learners, in this case.

As with other programmes using television, the A-plus programme typically had high development and production costs and low per user costs (less than US $0.10 per viewer per television programme). The annual costs of supporting a teacher in its Community Mobilisation Network was US $18 per teacher, and US $84 per school or institution. Similarly the development and transmission costs of interactive radio provision in South Africa's OLSET programme were low: US $1 per pupil per year and slightly more for teacher support. A similar picture emerges for Mongolia. The costs of radio are affected by the salary costs of producers and technicians in different countries and the regulatory framework affecting broadcasting. The cost of preparing transmitting and repeating a 20-minute national radio programme in Mongolia was US $110 but the cost of electricity for transmission was high and access to airtime for local radio stations was heavily regulated, limiting the use of local radio. In all of these cases, the delivery of television or radio programmes is not the end point but the beginning of other activities by teachers with the programme providers giving the support.

The use of distance education in at least one case allowed limited funds to be used in different and more effective ways. Whereas traditionally in Mongolia, 85 per cent of in-service funding for continuing professional development had been used for travel and substances, the use of distance education enabled a higher proportion of the budget to be used on the training element, that is, the certain of learning resources for teachers and more local workshops. This altered the amount of access teachers had to learning opportunities. Instead of one week's professional development per primary teacher once every ten years distance education enabled regular ongoing input through radio, printed materials and group meetings for over half of the country's teachers in six years. Given the range of professional development needs facing policy-makers and planners, new uses of available funds need to be explored if needs are to be met. Not all countries are in the position of Brazil where many opportunities and channels of provision for continuing professional development exist and at little or no cost to the teachers.

We are limited in the conclusions we can draw about costs. The data available in the case studies was often limited and partial for several reasons: cost data was not kept or known to the programme provider; information about costs was confidential or too sensitive to reveal or make public; costs were not recorded in ways which allowed the research to analyse the costs of the distance education programme; the complexity of the cost identification and analysis for some programmes was beyond the scope and time available for this study.

In pointing to the limited information on costs here, we also need to remember the similarly limited information on conventional teacher education programmes in many countries—one reason why the case researchers were not always able to draw comparisons. We also need to remember that the cheapest medium may or may not be the most appropriate one, so factors other than costs enter into media choices. One outcome of this exercise was that in several cases programme providers said that they were surprised at what they did not know about the costs of their own programmes and saw the need to improve their recording and analysis of costs, if they did. It might influence some of the choices made.

What media and technologies is it using?

Printed materials continue to be a mainstay of distance learning provision, even for programmes like the UK Open University's PGCE which has a major ICT element. Print plays a variety of roles, either as lead of supporting medium, and is valued for its durability, convenience, low cost, familiarity and suitability for combining with a variety of other media. Where print is the only medium available, especially for programmes focusing on teaching methodology, it has its limitations and can lack the immediacy of video or audio and the production process is slower than ICT delivery allows. Despite its familiarity, there is also scope for improvement in the design of self-study materials and existing textbooks are not always an adequate substitute though they have some role to play. In these ten cases, printed materials were used to varying extents in nearly all of the programmes in some way, the exception being the Chile case, where text materials were delivered on-line.

In two of these cases (OLSET South Africa and Mongolia) radio (with back-up audio-cassette use) has played a major role. It has provided an accessible, appropriate and low-cost technology, using a familiar medium in new ways to stimulate further activities. It can partner print effectively. In two cases (China and Brazil) television has been the main medium though used in very different ways. In China it was to deliver more formal talks or discussions or to show recordings, often made in studios, of classroom lessons taught by 'master teachers'. In Brazil it provided examples of applications in field settings with expert comment designed to challenge assumptions or stimulate argument as well as providing a core item around which other activities develop. In both cases, the countries have a strong infrastructure for television with educational channels available. Where radio and television are used, programmes often face the constraints of regulatory frameworks. In many countries, there is little enabling policy which facilitates the use of mass media for distance education and in some, the move to a market economy has eroded previous access.

Most cases relied on one or two main media plus face-to-face meetings; in some cases other media played a small role. Few combined several in an integrated way (the UK Open University case was unusual in doing this). No single medium can effectively provide (in a stimulating and illustrative way) the kinds of things teachers need to learn or see, especially when learning about teaching approaches and processes. Though there are great expectations of the role that ICT will play in teacher education, and though it opens up new possibilities, other media are capable of providing good quality teacher education programmes if well designed, appropriate, accessible and affordable. The use of ICT will grow gradually alongside other media use as infrastructure, costs and access make it more possible and is already playing a supplementary role in programmes. Because of the huge current interest in the use of ICT, we will explore its use in teacher education in the next section.

The use of ICT for teacher education

ICT in teacher education refers to two sets of activities or roles. One is training teachers to learn about ICT and its use in teaching as computers are introduced to schools. In many countries this is being done through face-to-face training programmes, often as part of initial teacher education. Some countries (such as the United Kingdom and Singapore) have developed policies which require all initial teacher education programmes to include compulsory courses in ICT as a strategy for building capacity in ICT. In other countries, no policy yet exists and teaching teachers about ICT is at best an option within teacher education programmes. In some cases, the facilities and equipment for supporting a strong policy are inadequate.

The other role of ICT is as a means of providing teacher education, either as a core or main component of a programme, or playing a supplementary role within it. The case of Chile illustrates both kinds of activities within one professional development programme; teachers on the programme learn to use ICT and to use it in teaching their different subjects by means of a wholly on-line programme which has, as its core element, on-line delivery and activities. In the case of UK Open University's initial teacher education programme, the materials are not delivered on-line, but on-line communication plays a key role in supporting student-teachers during school-based training, providing interaction with tutors and other students and feedback to programme providers.

Research and experience so far show that where ICT is offered as an optional supplement in programmes, it is less likely to be used by student-teachers than when it is a required activity for a purpose. As the Chile case showed, teachers who took the on-line version of the programme developed more use of virtual working environment than those on the face-to-face programme and developed a 'network communication culture'. So the outcomes of training programmes for teachers on the use of ICT appear to be affected by how the programmes are delivered. A common problem in programmes where ICT is a supplementary component is in getting students and tutors to use it.

In looking for established cases of ICT use for teacher education when planning this study, we found fewer than we expected. While many new initiatives have begun, there are few completed programmes with experience to report. There are many examples to be found of ICT forming part of a conventional programme of initial teacher education and whether this is a compulsory or optional part depends on government policy in a country. Sometimes this is taught as an on-campus subject or in some cases (as in Australia) it can be taken in an alternative distance learning mode. There were far fewer examples to be found of ICT as a core means of delivering or supporting initial teacher education programmes (not just ICT courses), especially in developing countries. There were more examples on on-line use for continuing professional development programmes at diplomas and higher degree level and for short courses. A great deal of activity is to be found at present in the use of ICT in providing informal professional development for teachers through on-line activities ('chat rooms', specialist subject conferences, virtual classrooms, networks, professional development websites, peer group discussions, bulletin boards, resource sharing). This gives teachers access to people and resources as well as putting more choices for professional development (formal and informal) into teachers' hands.

Out of experience so far some issues and lessons emerge for planners:

- Building teachers' capacity in ICT and using ICT as a means of teacher education and professional development cannot happen in isolation from its use elsewhere in the education system and wider environment.
- National policies, strategies and plans need to be integrated into the teacher education curriculum for initial teacher education and in priorities and funding allocation for continuing professional development.

- Teacher education cannot develop the use of ICT without the infrastructure and funding to support it and major investment and strong government policy is needed for this as the experience of some countries has shown (for example, Chile, the United Kingdom and Singapore).
- Experience shows too that teacher educators are a key element in establishing the use of ICT in education and teacher education but many teacher educators themselves lack skills and training in the use of ICT or the equipment to apply and develop their knowledge and skills, once gained.

The very limited evidence available on costs so far shows that, assuming an existing infrastructure, the development and teaching of on-line programmes may cost as much or more than face-to-face equivalents, though the cost structure will be different from that of face-to-face teaching or other kinds of distance education. Since students will often need to bear some of the costs, this may affect their access.

The advantages of ICT lie in its potential for increased interaction with and between learners, speedier delivery and response times to queries and feedback on assignments, greater access to communities of teachers and quicker lead-in terms for updating course materials while at the same time needing the establishment of effective quality assurance procedures. The use of ICT and CD-Roms, is becoming more common for materials developers of distance education programmes of all kinds and for supporting administrative processes and staff involved in tutoring or learner-support.

How is it managed?

Distance education programmes are provided through, a variety of organisational arrangements. Some are located in universities or institutions, some are provided through consortia or collaborations, and others are time-limited projects, often donor-funded. The categories of providers in this set of case studies are given in Table—2. Five of the programmes are made available through universities (for distance teaching universities and one traditional one). One programme is provided by a distance teaching teachers' college (an unusual form of institution). Three are donor-funded projects and one more is a programme provided by a consortium of private agencies, managed by the philanthropic division of a commercial, national communications network and privately funded.

Table—2 Types of providers

Category	*Case*
Universities	UNISA, South Africa
Distance-teaching university	Open University, UK China TV Teachers' college Indira Gandhi National Open University, India
Traditional university providing an on-line distance education programme	Universidad de la Frontera, Chile.
Distance teachers' college	National Teachers' Institute, Nigeria
Donor-funded projects	Open Learning System Education Trust, South Africa, with its own project structure and staff
	UNICEF in partnership with the Ministry of Science, Technology, Education and Training, and the School of Education Development (a national institute).
	RESAFAD (the African Network for Education at a Distance), Burkina Faso. A collaboration between several countries in West Africa and a development agency in France.
Consortium of private and public agencies	TV-Futura, Brazil

Some of the differences between the types of providers spring from different views about the role and functions of the state in educational provision. Brazil, for example, has a strong pluralist tradition which leaves space for the private sector to play a significant role in education. South Africa's ambitious reconstructionist aims can only be adequately met by a range of both governmental and non-governmental agencies. But there are strengths and limitations to operating outside the state educational system. The outsider status of TV-Futura and OLSET has given them independence from some political and pedagogical constraints that often accompany formal programmes. This has allowed them to research teachers' expressed needs more closely than many programmes offered by state providers and to create support for teachers of a directly practical nature, the sort of provision that is often unavailable through state provision. The private ownership of TV-Futura has also brought the benefits of high TV production standards. OLSET and TV-Futura have, with varying degrees of success, had to set up their own structures in curriculum development and materials production and in developing their outreach infrastructure. TV-Futura has had the benefit of high levels of private funding to develop an impressive outreach network. In contrast, the detached status of OLSET has led to a constant struggle for funding, particularly state funding, and for air-time on the national radio broadcasting station. This has often compromised the quality and consistency of its provision.

The donor-funded project is frequently used as a vehicle for teacher education but they have their strengths and limitations too. While they have more scope to innovate, bypassing the inertia of the traditional system, and demonstrating the feasibility of distance education, they are also more vulnerable, frequently dependent on external funding. Their, sustainability depends on whether the project, usually a time-limited initiative, becomes institutionalised. The history of distance education for teachers, especially in developing countries, is littered with the bones of short-term projects which have served their purpose and been discarded (until the next crisis in teacher education).

The established distance teaching universities have provided teacher education programmes alongside others. Through their regional infrastructures, they have increased access to programmes and professional development opportunities for teachers. They have administrative framework and logistical systems which can accommodate a range of different programmes and, sometimes, because systems are in place and shared, they can afford to run programmes that are not strictly cost-effective but are seen to have social worth (for example, the Certificate in Guidance programme. However, there are some challenges too: the provision of local support which is accessible, the monitoring and management of student support at the local level, the responsiveness of central providers to local differences or languages, the organisation and assessment of teachers' practical work, and the provision of timely feedback on student's coursework. Distance teaching universities may also have inflexible requirements as a way of ensuring standards. As a result, they may have inappropriate requirements for some non-formal programmes (as may be the case with the Certificate in Guidance or other similar programmes which do not fit neatly into an accreditation system). In addition, teacher education programmes often involve partnerships; with schools, local education officers, teachers' colleges, school inspectors, head-teachers and district authorities. In the case of initial teacher education, the management of courses and student progress is shared with partners such as those to varying degrees and especially in the management of practical teaching. In some cases responsibility is delegated altogether for the management of students' teaching practice (as in China). In others it is a specified and contractual partnership between the school and the distance education provider (as in the UK Open University). Most other arrangements fall somewhere between these two but, in all cases, they present challenges and have costs for a distance education provider.

How is it funded?

The case studies show that distance education for teachers receives funds from all four of the most usual sources of funds for education; from government budgets, from student fees, from the private and NGO sector and from funding agencies. Several programmes receive funding from a combination of sources so that, for example, the programmes in both China and Nigeria are funded partly by government, partly by student fees. Funding source is mapped onto the ten cases in Figure 1.

In general, governments have proved willing to fund not only initial teacher education, but also some programmes of continuing professional development, especially for curriculum reform, or for some upgrading programmes in countries trying to raise the minimum standard of teacher qualification. Students are often expected to pay fees where they enrol on a course which will benefit them in terms of career advancement or salary increment. The NGO sector is involved in the projects in Brazil and at OLSET in South Africa, but there are significant differences between the two. The provision in Brazil is through funds generated within the country by an established consortium, while OLSET is dependent on external donor funding and, despite its successes, seems unable to attract government funding. Like other long-term projects, questions about sustainability inevitably arise in relation to the future of the OLSET project and others like those in Mongolia where the support to in-service teacher education was intended as a temporary measure until the economic situation improved.

A number of policy issues emerge from the cases: how to find the appropriate balance between government funding and student fees for some kinds of teacher education programmes; the role distance education should play in both initial training and continuing professional development and in relation to conventional provision; how to maximise returns to training investment; where to locate responsibility for distance education within the education system; how to build a better information and evaluation basis for decision-making. In relation to policy formation, it can be said that distance education is not often considered enough as a strategic option when planning the provision of teacher education.

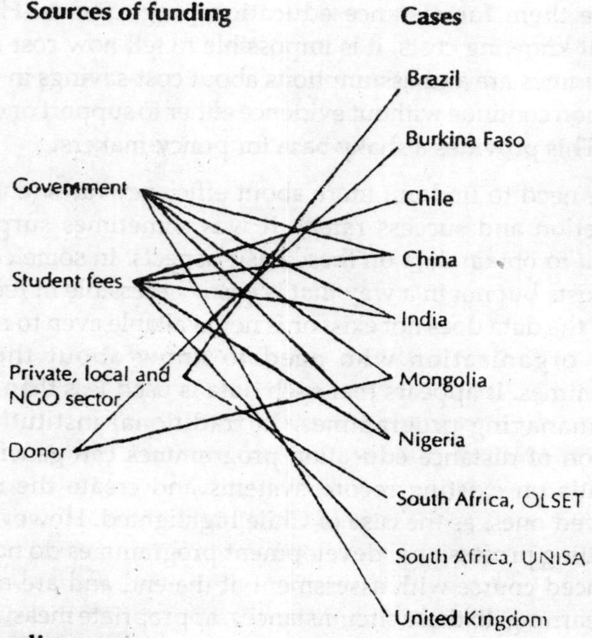

Fig. 1 Funding source

What do we still Need to Find out?

The ten case studies have provided a valuable resource which adds to our knowledge and understanding about the use of distance education for teacher education, both initial and continuing. They provide new studies, many of which have not previously appeared in the literature, and illustrate a range of different purposes, approaches and technologies. We reviewed key aspects of them in earlier parts of this report and finish now with one more. This is that the case studies have helped to highlight what we do not know and what we still need to find out.

We need to learn more about the costs of teacher education, whether conventional or distance education. Although the data on costs is slowly accumulating, this continues to be a neglected area. Some of the data is not available to the providers of distance education programmes, either because they have not recorded it at all, or in ways which would permit analysis. Some costs are known but confidential since they are a sensitive topic, and some providers are unwilling to reveal them. Some costs are not known because providers, though willing, are not sure how to record and analyse them for distance education programmes. However, without knowing costs, it is impossible to tell how cost-effective programmes are and assumptions about cost-savings in distance education continue without evidence either to support or disprove them. This provides a shaky base for policy-makers.

We need to find out more about efficiency rates (enrolment, completion and success rates). It was sometimes surprisingly difficult to obtain data on these basic aspects. In some cases, the data exists but not in a way that is easily accessible in records. In others, the data does not exist or is not available even to members of the organisation who need to know about their own programmes. It appears that such data is used less than it might be in managing programmes. In traditional institutions, the adoption of distance education programmes can generate new demands on existing record systems and create the need for improved ones, as the case of Chile highlighted. However, some continuing professional development programmes do not have a sequenced course with assessment at the end and are more like open learning. In these circumstances, appropriate measures need developing to find out what the participation rates are and what they signify and what kinds of record keeping would be both manageable and informative.

We need to know more about effectiveness and the impact of programmes on teaching and learning. For some distance education providers, their task ends at the point of delivery. For others, like Brazil's A-Plus programme, delivery is the starting point for further activities. So we need to learn more about different kinds of outcomes and the kinds of linkages between programmes and outcomes and the translation of things learned by teachers into improved teaching, and ultimately, improvements in children's learning. We also need to know more about the benefits and drawbacks of different options and outcomes in deploying resources and focussing effort in teacher education, not just within initial teacher education or continuing professional development, but in the balance between them. We need to keep monitoring and evaluating applications of ICT in teacher education in order to build a realistic picture of its strengths, limitations and costs and to identify effective strategies for introducing it.

We need to find out more about the policy environment of distance education for teacher education, both within teacher education and in relation to the wider environment of regulatory telecommunications or media policies. Some countries, in their policies and plans, have distance education as an explicit strategy for training teachers. Others have no mention of it and continue to think within the box of traditional models and customary allocation of resources while unable to meet pressing needs. Some of the traditional models no longer fit new needs. So we need to learn more about effective and enabling policies for the provision of teacher education using distance education.

Finally, we need to find out more about the evaluation of teacher education through distance education: the methods and approaches that would be most useful as well as manageable, the kinds of practices that already take place, the tools that would be useful and ways of evaluating programmes to take as much account of teachers' voices in remote village schools as of specialist curriculum developers in capital cities. As distance educators, we also need to find better ways of disseminating what we already know.

Index

T